$3.95

Honest Questions
Honest Answers

To Enrich Your Marriage

George & Margaret
HARDISTY

Honest Questions— Honest Answers

to enrich your marriage

By

George
and

Margaret Hardisty

For those who would like to sponsor a
FOREVER MY LOVE SEMINAR,
please contact:

Margie Ministries
3688 Mt. Diablo Blvd.
Lafayette, CA 94549

HONEST QUESTIONS—HONEST ANSWERS

Copyright © 1977 Harvest House Publishers
Irvine, California 92714
Library of Congress Catalog Card Number: 77-024828
ISBN 0-89081-039-7

Printed in the United States of America

DEDICATION

To our children, Vance and Elisa,
who consistently have been suppor-
tive of all our efforts to help others
and have gone out to do some
helping themselves, we lovingly
dedicate this book.

ACKNOWLEDGEMENTS

To the many pastors, psychiatrists, psychologists, priests and marriage counselors who have taken time to enthusiastically endorse our work, and share their knowledge; to relatives and friends whose lives made fascinating anecdotes; and to the host of new friends we have made throughout the world, we warmly offer our thanks. It has been a JOY having you touch our lives.

INTRODUCTION

Dear Husband . . . Dear Wife,

George came home last night shaking his head. It had been a crowded day: one family quarreling over a business venture; a mother and father offering their daughter's illegitimate child for adoption; a business executive who wanted to reconcile with his estranged wife; a young mother with four children under the age of six whose husband had just left her for another woman with children already past the diaper stage.

All in a day's work, but George realized once again why he has been willing, even anxious, to travel with me to deliver lectures and conduct seminars that have resulted from the widespread use of my book, *Forever My Love* (*What Every Man Should Know About His Wife*): We are trying to catch people upstream to help them before they are dashed on the marital rocks. I am continually grateful that he has consented to represent the male viewpoint so BOTH sexes would feel that SOMEONE cares and understands.

The long hours of travel, rushing to catch airplanes, stewing over luggage that sometimes gets shipped to the wrong place, going without meals, sleeping in strange quarters and the exhaustion resulting from it all, have been worth it as we have had the joy of meeting so many of you personally.

We have shared your fears and wept with you over your sorrows. We have been humbly grateful when you have taken the time to let us know that we had something to do with the healing of your hurts. We have rejoiced over your eagerness to help others by making sure our message has gone out to Uncle Jack, Aunt Penelope, Newlywed Ned, College Chris, and anyone else who needed it.

You have asked questions—lots of questions—and we have attempted to give you answers, many of which are contained herein. My husband has spent long hours writing his answers to your questions, so that I might blend them with mine. Our only regret is that, of necessity, we had to leave many in our files which we wanted to include.

It is our conviction that there is no problem that cannot ultimately be solved. It is our prayer that the solution to yours might be found in these pages. If so, send your thanks heavenward to God from Whom comes all help of lasting value.

Lovingly,

Margaret

CONTENTS

1

Sign Language

Good news! Whatever state your marriage is in, it can be improved. Is it broken? It can be mended. Is it wobbly? It can be made solid. Is it good? It can be better. Read on!

Where Did I Go Wrong?

Mark took a deep breath and blurted out what he hated to say—"Sherri is threatening to leave me."

Oh, there had been quarreling for several years over money, sex, housework and the rest. But he hadn't thought it was THAT bad. As Mark talked, his emotions played across his face: Embarrassment, confusion, perplexity, a bit of anger, fear and finally repentent regret as he admitted the mistakes he had made. The light from a nearby lamp accentuated the hurt in his eyes as he held out empty hands and asked, "Where did I go wrong?"

At the same time Mark was airing his griefs to George, a young wife searched my eyes pleadingly as she said, "Our marriage is blah. I feel like 'yuck' when Darryl comes near me."

She glanced at her handsome husband, who was listening and looking at her sadly. "I love him . . . I think." She shook her head, looking puzzled, and then asked, "What's happening? Why am I this way?"

Someone May Be Trying to Tell You

Sign language is fundamental to all relationships. Our Llasa-Maltese pressed his nose urgently on my leg. I looked down. He was a cute little fellow with his white hair framing his black eyes. His plumy tail dusted his back furiously as his nails clicked against the kitchen floor.

I went back to reading my recipe:

> Let's see . . . 2 cups of flour—click, click, click, click
> butter-hmmm-do I have enough?—click, click, click,
> salt   woops, spilled it—click, click, click, click, click

It was at the point when I couldn't remember whether or not I had put the baking powder in that I realized *SOMEONE was trying desperately to tell me something* and it was disturbing my concentration. When that someone continued to press his cold nose repeatedly against my leg, I finally whirled around, squatted down to his level and asked in exasperation, "What do you WANT?" Click, click, click, click—right to the door. Trying to keep the flour from dusting the latch, I opened it and he rushed outside to take care of his urgent need.

Our dog doesn't have a tongue that will form words. His reasoning process is definitely limited. His only recourse is to tell us what's bothering him by sounds and signs.

Usually before a marriage reaches a state of "limbo" or falls apart, SIGN LANGUAGE is all over the homestead.

We seem to figure if we just pretend that the sun is really shining when it isn't, the problems will somehow, someday, go away. Sometimes they do. But more often they don't.

Let's take a look at a few signs that spell T-R-O-U-B-L-E ahead in marriage:

STOP	Communication is stilted or nil.
CAUTION	One partner has started to turn off.
SLOW DOWN	You spend very little time together.
DETOUR	Partners are thinking more of what they can get rather than what they can give.
OPEN DITCH	Romance is not a daily part of your lives. It's been reduced to sex.
RED LIGHT FLASHING	You quarrel easily.
DON'T PASS	You haven't a vital relationship with God.
BUMPY ROAD	One of your children is becoming rebellious.
MUDDY ROAD AHEAD	You take each other for granted.
DANGER	You don't laugh much anymore.
CURVES	You lack patience and are critical.
LOOSE GRAVEL	You don't look forward to seeing each other every day.
WRONG WAY	You respond rudely when your mate asks you something.
TUNNEL	You feel sorry for yourself.

Warning signs! It's time to take a good look at them and pay attention to what they say.

2

A Woman Is What A Man Does

ALL IT TAKES IS A LITTLE UNDERSTANDING

We had just finished our lecture and the crowd was beginning to mill around. We both spotted him at the same time: a big, burly fellow with a very stern look on his face, headed straight for us. We didn't know whether to duck, run, or throw a body block. Before we were able to cut loose from indecision, he boomed out,

> *I spend 14 hours a day making sure my business is a success. I think you're right. I ought to spend a few minutes each day making sure my marriage is a success, too! How do I do it?*

Just then two other couples who had accompanied him and his wife to the dinner, joined us and one of the men interjected:

> *You mentioned that a man meets life with his head. A woman with her heart. What do you mean?*

Three men. Two questions. Twelve eager, hopeful eyes wanting instant instructions on how to bake a perfect cake when we hadn't even been told what ingredients were available for our use. So, although there was no way we could give them a finished product in those late evening hours, we began with some basic concepts which we hoped would open their understanding and get them started on a new and vital approach to their marriage difficulties.

We repeat those basic concepts in this chapter simply because they will make our reasons for subsequent answers clearer and more understandable to you. If you have read my book, *Forever My Love*, you will be able to build further on the firm foundation you have begun.

BOTH women and men have been asking us questions right and left and it's for sure, BOTH need help. BOTH sexes are suffering from unpleasant-mates disease and NEITHER sex is totally at fault in most cases.

If you haven't read *Forever My Love*, these thoughts may be new to you. But they just might give you the push you need to start putting that WHOOPEE back into your life that has been missing for quite awhile.

Sexy Or Else

When we asked a man recently how he was going to be sure his second marriage worked, he replied, "Simple. She's going to be sexy and ready to go whenever I say."

In his thinking, SHE is responsible as to whether their marriage makes it or not, and her responsibility will center in the bedroom. He comes by his expectations honestly. The market is flooded with admonitions to women on how to be alluring to a man so he will look more than twice, how to hook a husband, how to hang on to a husband, how to get rid of a husband . . . you name it, the presses have been rolling out that kind of material for years!

Women are so anxious to arouse the proper response in the men around them that they search diligently for anything on that subject that comes along, whether it be a book, magazine article, TV or radio talk show or self-improvement course. And the majority seem to come up with one answer: "SHAPE UP, LADY. Get sexy. Be a whiz of a housekeeper. Become Supermother. Knuckle under and you won't have to worry about losing your man." The women go at it tooth and nail, but the fact remains that the divorce courts are working overtime to keep up with the load and in some areas there are more divorces per year than weddings!

The Hidden Key

In our years of counseling others, George and I have discovered an important truth: The wife has been stumbling around since the honeymoon days, looking for a key that will fit the lock that opens the door to marital bliss. And all along, the key has been hidden in someone's pocket—the husband's. And only with great difficulty can she lift that heavy key out of his pocket and make it work.

Let me explain. Every woman is *different* from any other woman ever created. But there is one basic way she and all the others out there are alike—she approaches life from an emotional plane where her relationship with her man is concerned. His knowledge of this weakness is his KEY to a happy marital relationship.

To explain it further. The woman wants to be the "everything" in her man's life. She wants to be the sugar in his coffee, the salt in his casserole. She prefers to believe that when he is hard at work, he is frequently, if not constantly, thinking of her and longing to be home with her. She has to believe that he would never THINK of entertaining thoughts about another woman, that he couldn't bear to have anyone but her. She needs him to be protective and yet allow her to be independent.

She depends upon him to make her feel beautiful, gifted, precious and deeply loved.

If he supplies this emotional need, it will give him the power necessary to have her practically worshipping at his feet, adoring him and wanting to serve him.

The formula works like this:

> MAN HOLDS KEY (his knowledge of woman's need)
> HE PUTS KEY IN LOCK (supplies her needs)
> KEY OPENS DOOR TO MARITAL HAPPINESS
> (he finds it her nature to respond and give back more than she receives)

Thus we find the meaning behind the biblical injunction, ". . . husbands, dwell with them according to knowledge, giving honor unto the wife as unto the weaker vessel, and as being heirs together of the grace of life, that your prayers be not hindered."

Everything But What She Needed

After speaking to a women's luncheon, I was approached by two women who were dripping with jewels, expensive perfume, makeup and furs. They wanted to talk. Could I? Before long we were traveling to an out of the way place. Since it has not been my windfall to travel in "those" circles, I wasn't sure whether I was in a Rolls Royce or not. It certainly did smell like one.

As we dawdled over orange juice, the most attractive one of the two poured out her heart. She loved her husband and she knew he loved her. She had an unlimited bank account (her hobby was playing around with expensive paintings and art objects). She had recently taken a trip around the world with several lady friends, and had enjoyed the attention of other men so much that she was considering having an affair with a playboy she met. When I asked her why she would risk losing her husband, she said, "I don't want to lose him. I just want to shake him up. He never gives me any real attention. When he looks at me, his mind is still back in his office counting the next million." He gave her everything but what she really needed: more of himself.

That brings us to a question which has been asked of us from California to New York by men who sincerely want to take a leadership role in improving their marriages:

How can I fulfill my wife's emotional needs?

To a woman little things mean a lot. Little things, like what's coming up next!

ROMANCE . . . IT'S NOT WHAT YOU THINK

One confused but well meaning husband commented:

I try to romance my wife but she resists my advances!

SAME WORD. DIFFERENT MEANING. He was thinking of sex. That's not romance to your wife. To her, sex is only the *end result* of romance from time to time. To her, ROMANCE is tender, loving care from you, ALL the time. It is *more* than dinner out once in awhile. Romance is your complimenting her on her looks, her cooking, her housekeeping, her brains, on anything she does! It's when you DON'T criticize her. What do you do when she cries? Get hard? Or think she's a prima donna? A romantic holds his wife closely and says (even if he has done nothing wrong), "I'm sorry."

Romance is when a man says to a woman, "You're a doll, you're beautiful, you're the only one in the world for me." It's a touch of the hair as you go by . . . uhhh . . . gently. It's when you reach over and squeeze her hand in church. It's helping her on with her coat and opening doors for her. It's when you leave a note on the bathroom mirror or call her two or three times during the week from work, ''Just because I was thinking of you.''

Romance is a gift from you that she wouldn't buy for herself, like a music box or a special teacup. It's ''unspecial day'' gifts like a rose, or a box of pretty soaps. Romance is telling her you love her, a MINIMUM of once a day. It's taking her out to dinner to a really nice place even if you have to save up your nickels to do it.

One husband asked me what in the world he could buy for his wife's birthday since funds were short. The result was that he borrowed a lovely little basket (the type where you lay a colorful napkin over the top), purchased all sorts of goodies from a delicatessen, got a babysitter for their son and took her to a lovely spot by a lake for a surprise picnic. That's romance. Next time, hopefully, he'll think of something himself.

One radio host who interviewed me on a talk show shared, ''I decided to try some of that stuff with my wife. I couldn't believe what happened! I've been married 23 years and I thought I knew everything about her. But, all of a sudden, I've got a new, exciting woman. It's like a miracle.''

More Important Than Gifts—Attention!

Several women have complained:

> *TV is coming between us. I feel like second choice.*

TV can be exasperating, so why not do a switcharound? Quit nagging and join him. You can knit, balance your checkbook, or crack walnuts. Just keep busy in front of the TV so you don't get frustrated and irritated. When he turns off the set suggest you both step outside for a breath of fresh air. Talk about happy things: the moon, the flowers, the grass. Or maybe don't talk at all. Just hold his hand, tugging a little so he'll walk. If he won't go outside, be vivacious and interesting inside! If you have kept up your knowledge by reading or pursuing a fascinating hobby, and you share these things with him, he might even find there is more fun in you than in the tube. And after all, there is! *Isn't* there?

He Should Know!

A typical female reaction is this one from Texas:

I have to remind my husband of things he should be doing, like telling me he loves me. But I want it to be sincere and spontaneous.

Many couples don't come right out and let each other KNOW what's bothering them. A man is often bewildered at his wife's anger because she didn't tell him what was getting to her. Coupled with kindness and gentleness, laying it on the line is the first step that some people should take. But failing in that, the next step is to compensate.

When a husband forgets the nice words that make life beautiful for his wife, *she* should use them on *him*. When she says, in a quiet moment, "I love you" and waits without success for him to return the favor, she can turn away, glance back at him with a twinkle and a smile and say, "I don't think I heard you tell me that you loved me." Then if he responds affirmatively, she can hold him close for a moment and whisper, "Thanks. I need to hear that often. That's the woman in me."

Please Tell Me

Yes, words are extremely important to the female sex. We've seen pretty women become very attractive and unattractive women become very lovely, depending on what is going on INSIDE. One little wife in New Jersey asked,

Why do I feel so inferior because I'm not a perfect specimen of a woman physically?

She was right. She was not a perfect specimen. In fact, she was far from it. Further discussion revealed that her husband had never told her he thought her attractive or that he loved her. We couldn't guarantee he would change, but we encouraged *her* to change, and to start with her *thinking*. We shared with her the story of a woman we know who is 86 years old. Physically, she is not what one would call a pretty woman. Photos from her past reveal that she never was. In fact, she was homely. But this woman had been married twice—to two very handsome men, both of whom died. Just in the past 15 years, she has received three marriage proposals! People of all ages, including youngsters, love to be around her. She is vibrant, interesting, capable and gifted. Her house is always full of flowers and gifts from admirers. She keeps herself beautiful by thinking *positively*, believing in *herself* and *reaching out to others to help them*.

She Floors Him

An exasperated husband from Virginia blurted out:

My wife gets overly emotional. What's with her? If I say anything nice to her, she's all over me. So I don't say anything nice.

His wife was standing behind him, listening and bursting with life. She was beautiful to look at and a delightful conversationalist. She agreed that he was telling it like it was. Since she usually had to draw every compliment out of him, she was trying to encourage him when he did do it on his own. As a result, when the poor fellow did venture out a bit she was so thrilled she virtually attacked! Our suggestion was that he make a deal with her: He would make an effort to say nice things to her every day, if she would promise to accept them more quietly.

She Won't

It hasn't been very surprising to us when men report that they've tried romance at our suggestion and they like it! In fact, some complain because the *wife* is the one who drags her feet. Like Jerry:

> *How do you convince a wife that a honeymoon [once or twice a year] away from the kids, would be rewarding? Her main objection is the safety of kids and pets. She feels she would worry so much she wouldn't have a good time.*

I can identify with her. I never wanted to leave the children for more than a few hours. I feared for their safety. But George insisted. Although we haven't done it often, the times we did were wonderful. For him, it was a welcome break from the problems of other people that always weigh on an attorney, and the constant ringing of the telephone demanding his attention. For me, it was fantastic just to have my husband's undivided attention while we swam, lolled in the sun or ate a delicious dinner.

Your wife may believe that there is no one else capable of doing her job right. Some women fear their children and pets will find that MOTHER isn't the whole world. Their insecurity is showing. Actually, giving children a breather from the hovering parental PRESENCE is good! They'll appreciate you all the more when you come back and will tend to develop more rounded lives.

Regarding worry, here is top grade psychology:

"Be anxious for nothing; but in everything, by prayer and supplication with thanksgiving, let your requests be made known unto God. And the peace of God which passeth all understanding, shall keep your hearts and minds through Christ Jesus."

Once you insist she goes on that "honeymoon," she'll have a good time, never fear. And how's this for some advice from my own King of Romance himself—my husband:

"Draw love notes in the sand. Sit, uninterrupted, by candlelight as you build memories. Throw snowballs and laugh. Find a secret place by a bubbling stream where you can share your innermost thoughts. Children and pets are ours only for awhile, but husband and wife are until death do them part."

No Time

Men write:

We can't find time to get alone.
or
We're so busy doing the Lord's work, there's no time to share tender moments.

You have as much time as everyone else: 24 hours a day. You manage to do the things you regard as important and essential to life, don't you? How important is your marriage relationship? Consider how you would feel if your partner was taken from you, or worse, left you. Would you do like some and beg us for answers on how to get her back?

Many people fall for that old ploy of the enemy which tells us that we just can't say no to people, to organizations or to the "Lord's work." George and I have found that not every opportunity of service is sent from the Lord. When we receive 20 invitations to speak on the same night, obviously 19 of them aren't issued from heaven!

Review your time at least twice a year and budget it, like money, setting definite evenings aside for each other and your family. If someone asks for that time, you can honestly say, "We have a previous engagement."

We have had to stop and evaluate *our* lives frequently. This past year we have been very involved in traveling, lecturing, conducting seminars and writing, as well as in our regular occupations. We were finding less and less time to just enjoy each other, even though we were together a great deal. One evening, George informed me that things were going to change, starting RIGHT NOW! It was late, but we dressed up in our finery, went out to do some window shopping, bounced around on some waterbeds in a store that was still open, and then enjoyed a leisurely dinner in a restaurant that was quiet and heavy on atmosphere. We talked and talked and forgot temporarily that there was work tomorrow and we had schedules to keep. We enjoyed that evening so much!

Just Can't Leave

Several farmers have stated a similar concern, like this dairyman:

> *I can't get away alone with my wife. The animals can't be left and our livelihood depends on them.*

If you can't afford to hire someone for a few days to take care of your animals, or whatever, you and your wife can have what we call MINI-VACATIONS together. Pack a picnic lunch and go to a lovely spot on your farm where you can be alone for a couple of hours. Saddle the old mare and ride off together—just for fun. Take walks and just talk. Dress up in your best suit for a candle-lit dinner (which *you* bought in town at a delicatessen) for the two of you after the children go to bed. (That's in addition to the occasional dinner out together.) Consider putting aside a separate fund for that hired help so you can get away together, without the children, for a weekend or a whole week. It's more important than an extra chicken brooder!

Romance is as essential to a woman as breathing, almost. A woman who had read an interview with me in a newspaper immediately got my book, read it carefully, gave it to her husband to read, and wrote, "I just wanted to tell you that you saved our marriage. When my husband read your message, he did an about-face. We have stopped our divorce and fired our psychiatrist!" Not every person is willing to change overnight, as in that case, but a wise husband will start practicing romance on a daily basis until it becomes a part of his natural way of doing things. When men take the lead by supplying their wives' needs, the women respond in the most astounding ways, and happy husbands continue to tell us they only wish they'd started years ago!

Smart women work at romance, too, keeping nice things happening in their homes, regardless of what Papa does. He needs romance, too, whether he realizes it or not.

But romance isn't the *only* way to supply your sweetheart's emotional needs. Read on!

LET HER OUT OF THE COCOON

Her owl-like glasses perched stylishly on her nose seemed unusually large. It was apparent that her preferred hairdo had something to do with the impression—she had pulled it back in a bun which looked as if it hadn't been baked long enough. It made her appear small and somehow vulnerable. She was a reporter, a young woman determined to make it in life her way. She was a feminist. She believed in Women's Lib. She interviewed me because she had read that I was urging men to let their women develop as individuals.

However, she made it most clear that there was no man in her life, nor was there ever going to be. Men made slaves of women, she felt. They took advantage of them.

The interview lasted two hours. I presented my views. As we talked, the no-nonsense eyes behind the owlies began to soften. As I stood up to go, she suddenly smiled. And just as suddenly, she was pretty. In typical feminine fashion, and not at all in keeping with her chosen self-portrait, she clutched her hands, gave a little bounce, and said, "I can hardly wait to go out and find a man who will treat me like that!"

Hopefully, she will be fortunate enough to marry one who will be romantic and willing to do whatever he can to kiss away every doubt she ever had. And if he is very wise, he will urge her to continue developing in her chosen field. And if *she* is very wise, even after the children start to come she will keep in touch with her profession.

Women's Lib?

> *Don't you think that divorces are being caused by wo-*
> *men working outside the home?*

It all meshes together. To over-simplify a very complicated sociological trend, we can sum up a lot of life experiences by saying: Divorce isn't caused necessarily by women working outside the home. The eroding process began IN the home. The work outside the home merely hastens the process, sometimes, if the home situation isn't corrected. When a woman is being mistreated, or her life is devoid of romance; when she begins to feel used as a sex object or a workhorse; when she isn't encouraged to be anything but a flower growing in her husband's shadow, the world looks mighty tempting. Out she goes, seeking what she should have been receiving at home from her husband. Once out there, she receives a measure of respect, men flirt with her and make her feel attractive, she is able to accomplish something special in her job and is not taken for granted. At least that's what she *thinks* it will be like.

Sometimes it is. Very often it isn't.

Women are re-evaluating their positions and finding them not all bad. A husband needs to work with his wife, encouraging her to reach out and develop herself, and then a woman's position becomes very fulfilling.

The Matzos Jar

> *"What do you mean?" shouted one husband. "The Bible says that women are to stay at home."*

He was referring to Titus 2:5. But let's back up one verse and read: ". . . that they may encourage the young women to love their husbands, to love their children, to be sensible, pure, workers at home, kind, being subject to their own husbands, that the word of God may not be dishonored."

One of the greatest dangers in reading the Word of God is taking one verse and hanging the world on it. False religions and cults start that way. So do serious problems in marital relationships. To find the real meaning of a verse we have to compare it with additional scripture. In this case we may go to Proverbs 31, where we read about God's ideal wife. Here's a woman who was truly a worker at home, ruling and managing wisely and then going forth to exercise her special gifts. She had a business head and she used it. She was able to make money by buying property and improving it. She was clever with her hands, so she set up a mini-girdle factory at home. To those intimate items, she added exquisite linen she had made and put her products on consignment in one of the most fashionable markets in town. She realized a tidy profit from that venture, as well as from her real estate successes, which she hid in her matzos jar to be taken out for special uses.

She must have had a wonderful time shopping for gifts for her husband since she could buy things for him with money she made herself. And what joy it gave her to decide where she was going to spend her tithe—the 10% plus required by the Lord. She was especially fond of helping the poor around her with it.

Examine the passage carefully. Despite all her activities outside her home, she was a superb manager *at* home. No, her husband didn't try to hold this great lady down and keep her in the kitchen making unleavened bread. He was benefiting from the talents of this remarkable person who roamed hither and yon to conduct her various enterprises. He adored her, he praised her, and the children followed suit.

But Some Men Are Worried

Doesn't a woman who is pursuing a full-time career get more and more independent? Doesn't this sometimes contribute toward unhappiness in marriage?

Independence of a woman doesn't have to mean unhappiness if the husband takes it as something to admire and respect. If he delights in the stories she has to relate and shares in her successes just as she does in his, together they will be two exciting, wonderful people enriching each other's lives immeasurably.

Of course, when a woman has a career that takes her away from her husband and children in the evening and weekend hours (except occasionally) she can't very well be a good manager at home. She may wake up someday to find that she has sacrificed the things that were most important to her. We caution these women to be careful that the excitement and glamour of a job isn't just the lure of an unseen enemy trying to break up her life.

How?

Men and women who are getting this message and wanting to do something about it are asking ''Where do we start?'' Some women, when first let out of the pumpkin shell, blink at the bright light, confused and disoriented. They try to reach out but they fail.

One wrote:

> *I know I am capable of doing the things I want to do to improve myself, but I seem to always let a defeatist and self-pitying attitude get in my way. I quit before I begin.*

Whether you are the wife of a pastor, a bricklayer, a doctor or a candlestick maker, our message is the same. Your talents weren't meant to be hidden, and neither were you.

Any husband can encourage this type of wife by:

- complimenting her consistently on what she accomplishes, assuring her continually that she CAN do it and will be one of the best.
- helping her get work out of the way so she is free to turn her thoughts toward her special project.
- encouraging her to get it done.
- insisting she take the time necessary to reach her goals.

Her Own Business?

> *Should Christian women be more assertive in matters of business dealings? For instance, should I start my own business?*

Why not? If you have the capital and the know-how, get your courage from Proverbs 31 and branch out. You could make your husband the happiest man in town. We have known of more than one woman who, because they had the freedom to decide, (because they had mature husbands), made their husbands millionaires by clever investments.

Treated Like a Child

Here's an example of the kind of thing that drives women into a shell or out of the house. An indignant wife demanded to know:

> *Should a husband plan his wife's day for her? Should a husband pick his wife's friends? Do I owe my husband a minute-by-minute account of my day's work activities?*

The answer is "NO" on all three counts, of course. It looks as if your husband has you mixed up with the children. He is to honor you, not put the unbearable burden of totalitarian rule on your back.

But there's no need to throw up your hands and quit. You can beat him at his own game:

1) Develop a sweet, loving attitude toward him at all times. Avoid temper flare-ups.

2) Firmly take your stand. Have a serious talk with him. Tell him you love him and want him to always respect you as a mature person. But there is no way he can respect you if you allow him to treat you like a child.

3) Point out that, before you were married, you were able to plan your day, choose your friends and that not even your parents expected to know every single thing you did during the day.

4) Assure him that you will probably want to share with him, if he is interested because he loves you and wants to be part of you. But the desire to be a dictator or to distrust you is not valid.

5) Start acting mature, trustworthy and responsible. If there are things you do that obviously irritate him (like not having the house in order), then change.

Honor Not Bully

What does it mean to honor my wife?

What if your *boss's* wife requested to stay with you and your wife for a few days while her husband was out of town? How much honor would you show her? *Pulllenteee!* How come you'd treat your boss's wife better than *your* wife? Hmmm? The answer comes, "My job! That's why! Money! I need both or I *will* be neglecting my wife." Agreed! Your job and money are important, without a doubt. Continue showing honor to your boss's wife. Now, what about *your* wife? How important do you think *she* is? Honor is a strong word, and a command from God.

Now For the Juggling

Where is a working wife's place in the home?

If the children are small, it would be better if the wife didn't leave the home to work, even if it means scrimping in some areas. They need her. Part-time jobs are good if the children are school-aged, but she should be home by the time they get in from school.

I remember a bright little boy from years ago when I taught fifth grade. In class he was no problem, but after school I wasn't sure what to do with him. His mother worked and he was on his own for several hours. He would hang around until he was forced to leave (school rules). He had convinced himself that he was madly in love with me. When a young male teacher would show me attention, his jealousy was a thing to behold. He needed his mother!

If SOMEONE had been assigned to take mother's place until she could make it home, he wouldn't have wandered hither and yon seeking for that substitute. Many teenagers wouldn't become problems either, if there was someone home each afternoon who cared and they were expected to be home, too.

If the mother does work, however, and she has made sure her children are adequately cared for, she and her husband can make their times with the children especially pleasant and special.

Evening and weekend work at home should be shared by the husband. Her day is just as long as his.

Then There Are The Other Women

How does a Christian employer cope with women and their desire to be equal with men in management?

Even though many women in business would deny they have ANY needs where men are concerned, you can go on the assumption they all do and treat them accordingly. Politeness, kindness, a patient "I-want-to-listen-to-you-because-you-have-something-important-to-say" attitude are all essential in dealing with women employees. That doesn't mean you have to give in to all their demands. But consider them carefully. Weigh their thinking as fairly as you do that of the men, or even if it is contrary to what has always been company policy. You might find some solid ideas coming from the women that will push your company ahead.

Some women, like some men, would make excellent managers. Others would be picky, finicky and generally a pain-in-the-neck just like their male counterparts. Choose them carefully, but don't be afraid to use them.

By the way, married and middle-aged women often make far better employees than the single girl who is hired because she's a nice decoration. They are more dependable, oftentimes, and they know how to put in a solid day's work. They won't generally take time off pretending to be sick because they've got a heavy date. We like the fact, too, that some companies are starting to stagger a woman's work hours so that either she or her husband can be home when the children get there. Our nation is at stake on that issue. If the nation goes down the tube because the children are shifting for themselves, your business will go down right along with it.

IT'S WORKING!

It's one thing to AGREE to what one should be doing, but it's quite another to get it done. Many men say to us, like Tim did:

> If I started doing these things my wife would think I was nuts!

How do you know? Have you given it a good go? One client of George's contacted him and said, "I tried it. It didn't work." "How long did you try it?" George asked. "Ten days," he replied. "She didn't respond, so I gave up." Ten days! Twelve years went by before he tried anything positive. Twelve years of breaking down a marriage. Now he expects it to be built up in ten days?

Women and men who have been hurt deeply don't respond to sudden kindness easily. They're afraid they'll be hurt *worse* if they do. A man with a wounded wife needs to try for six months, or a year, or five years—whatever is necessary to rebuild the relationship. If he is sincere in wanting to win back her love, he can do it. It is the same with women who have turned-off husbands. We get practical about this in Chapter 13—*When Love, Trust or Respect Is Gone.*

We have been astounded at the number of men and women who have let us know that our methods *have* worked. One internationally known Christian leader wrote, "We didn't have a BAD marriage, but it certainly wasn't ideal, either. When I read your book, the Lord convicted me quickly and deeply. I realized that I had completely missed the boat where my wife was concerned. I did an about-face and, well, I just want you to know it has revolutionized our marriage."

When men switch horses in midstream they don't always get positive reactions from their ladies. After nine years of bickering with his wife, fighting for position in the home, nearly divorcing several times, Brad decided to try the romance bit. He placed a rose by Cynthia's pillow when he left for work (she had long ago decided she didn't want to please *him* with little things like making his breakfast). A week or so later he helped her on with her coat. She didn't say a word either time. He got discouraged. When we asked her why she didn't comment, she replied, "I don't think it'll last. I'll just wait and see."

Never Satisfied

Other women tell their men to "knock off that stuff" when actually they're deeply touched inside, but don't want to have to give up the anger they have been cherishing against their husbands. Others act most ungraciously. A husband in California has that problem:

> *So I gave her some gifts. But everytime she just looks disappointed and says, "I wanted something else" instead of accepting it in love.*

For many years, I did a slow burn or a hot blow-up when I would shop lovingly and painstakingly for "just the right thing" for George, only to have him trot right downtown the next week and return it. Actually, it was partially my fault because I KNEW what he really liked to receive was a wrench, a new ladder or some other "non-attorney-like" thing. But what really would do me in was when he blithely would walk into a store six months later and buy the very same item that he didn't keep! No amount of chiding or getting upset changed his mind. If he didn't like it when he received it, he didn't keep it.

To be completely fair, he didn't originate the idea. His mother felt it was a waste of money to receive things she didn't like or couldn't use and she taught her children that. In some ways I have to admit it has its merits, especially in as affluent a society as ours.

So we have compromised. He makes a list, with perhaps 20 things on it of all prices. I choose one or more, depending on my budget at the time. At least he's a *little* surprised, because he doesn't know which ones I'll choose.

Another fellow who decided to become a knight in shining armor had this difficulty:

> *What if your wife just says "Who are you kidding"*
> *when I compliment her or use affectionate words? And*
> *how do I get her to use terms like "honey?"*

Here's a woman who may not have seen much affection expressed in her home when she was a child. Criticism may have been the order of the day instead of praise. She needs educating like some teenagers who come to our home. As you are aware, teenagers can't seem to react well when you comment, "How nice you look today," or "I heard you did a great job!" You get all kinds of dumb responses ranging from a hyena's laugh to a long dissertation on how awful they really look and how terrible they actually did. When that happens, we just say to them, with a twinkle, "All you have to do is say, 'Thank you'." They soon get the point and start responding humanly, developing some poise in the process. Use the same tactics with your wife, assuring her that if you didn't mean it you wouldn't say it.

Furthermore, if she hears you say "honey," "sweetheart," "precious," and the like frequently, she might start picking up those terms and using them herself without feeling self-conscious. If not, when you are cuddling her in front of the fire some night, ask her to use sweet words when she talks with you because it makes you feel needed and cared for. Her motherly instinct shouldn't be able to resist that one.

The Games We Play

This question may have come from one of those fellow's wives:

> *If you are constantly receiving little compliments from your mate, doesn't it turn into more of a game than a true communication, causing mistrust: never knowing if your partner really means what he is saying?*

What is "true communication?" Is it this? "I'll say what *I* want when *I* want to and if I *have* to put *my*self out to say what I don't *want* to say, I am playing a game." Or conversely: "You are saying nice things. Therefore, *I* must be suspicious because *I* have learned not to trust people. You couldn't possibly be sincere." I've found that most people have no trouble expressing themselves loud and long on what they *don't* like and in using *negative* communication.

King "I" rules our lives. If King "I" were dethroned there would be much less trouble in marriages today. Learn to trust and accept from other people. By throwing up defenses you actually get bruised more easily because quarreling, alienation and unhappiness follow in the wake of that type of sailing. So someone takes advantage of you once in a while, or laughs at you? What of it? The important thing is that you don't do the same to someone else and as you accept their love they'll begin to enjoy giving it.

P.S. from Margaret: Men, you don't know what marvelous, clever, able creatures you are. Within your reach is the ability to set your wife's heart racing with excitement and adoration. And when you see THAT happening, yours will race, too. Put two racing hearts together and what have you got? Ummmmmmmm.

3

Sex, The Bedroom Battle

SHE'S RESISTING AGAIN!

We received this comment from Missouri:

We thank you from the bottom of our hearts. You've helped us solve our sex problems.

Success in the bed means that you *don't* start in the bedroom. The man carries the major weight of the load. He is the pursuer, she the pursued. And if he wants success, he will pursue her the way she likes it. That means romance (her brand. See Chapter Two, *Romance—It's Not What You Think*) morning, noon and night, yesterday, today and tomorrow—in other words, all the time. Then when the lovemaking begins, the field has been plowed and the major part of the job has been done.

It is amazing, though, how few men really catch on to this OBVIOUS truth, even though they seemed to know how to treat women BEFORE they married.

She's Turned Off

One fellow stated indignantly,

What about what makes ME happy? I want sex, so she should give it to me.

His wife is turned off and resists his advances. We would like to turn his comment around and put it the way he SHOULD be stating it.

I want sex. But my wife is a tender, sensitive creature. If I treat her as if she were a machine, purely for my comfort, she'll begin to hate my advances. I want her to enjoy sex. If she enjoys it, I will enjoy it more, too. So, I will treat her as that tender, sensitive creature, supplying her needs and then she will gladly supply mine.

But the battle rages on, because people *take* with very little thought of *giving*. Men are not wrong to *desire* their wives, of course. God invented sex and sanctioned it within the marriage bonds. But He never intended men to *use* women, in or out of marriage.

Men are forever going about doing the wrong things it seems. This fellow is one of them:

After six years, my wife is totally 'turned off' to sex. I've even considered using sex helpers. And I've wondered if I could turn another woman on. I feel so dead. What can I do?

We sent him a detailed plan which you can find in Chapter 13, *How To Win Your Wife Back*, and wrote, "You have to start all over again with a wife like this, hearkening back to the joyful times she experienced with you when you were dating her. The sooner you get going, the better."

Men Ask, "What Turns a Woman Off?"

Okay, here they are—a few of the obvious and most common violations by the best turner-offers in the business:

- burping out loud (and other poor table manners)
- poking at her intimate parts when you approach her
- criticizing her when you seldom praise her
- being romantic and nice only when you want sex
- clamming up and not listening when she needs to talk with you
- not keeping things up around the house (like oiling squeaky hinges)
- abusing her physically or verbally
- not trusting her in areas of responsibility
- using cutting remarks, in jest or not in jest
- not complimenting her on her cooking, her housekeeping, looks, etc.
- not using expressions like "I love you" or "You're a doll."
- wearing dirty, sloppy clothes around the house (unless you are working at a dirty, sloppy job)
- not keeping clean and free of odor
- showing interest in other women
- using foul language or dirty talk
- expecting her to submit to unorthodox methods of sex
- taking her for granted

I'm sure there are more YOUR wife could add to the list. Maybe you had better ask her to do so. Sex is pretty important, and if you aren't making it there, you aren't going to have a very happy life together.

Is That ALL They Think About?

Women ask: ARE MEN BLIND TO OTHER EMOTIONS BESIDES SEX?

Men have sensitive emotions, but when it comes to women, sex is mainly what enters their thinking. Widespread pornography doesn't help and is, indeed, causing men to become even more insensitive to women's needs, which compounds marital problems. But a man can let light and beauty rule his relationship with his wife instead of the darkness of selfishness.

Not Tonight

One of the most serious hindrances to harmony in any part of the home is poor health. Its spectre haunts the bedroom as well. Many a man has called his "tired" wife an excuse-maker. Too many women have been labeled "frigid" because they couldn't respond. So much misery and resentment could be prevented if these clay houses we live in were in tip-top shape.

A disgusted husband asks:

> *What about the wife who wants to sleep all the time?*
> *This must always be first—then sex.*

She's weary. Have you two considered having some romantic times during the daytime? If you can't do it during the week, send your children to someone's house for a few hours on Saturday or Sunday while you go out to a nice lunch or have one at home, ending up with lovemaking.

Consider this, too: Are you helping your wife with the evening work? A fifteen-hour day is too much for her. And how about a complete physical? When was the last time she had one?

Too Much Is Enough

One young man whose wife left him got in touch with us and said, "Now I understand what you were saying. As I look back,

I can see what I did wrong. It was always, 'I have my rights and you had better give them to me or else.' I never considered her feelings.''

This woman was ready to walk out on her husband:

> *He insists on sex every night and sometimes in the morning. He won't get a job and I work long hours. By bedtime I'm dead tired. Do I have to submit to all this? He does this just to satisfy himself—nothing more.*

How often we have heard, "Wives, you must submit to your husbands, no matter what!" But seldom do we hear anyone saying to the husband, "Husbands, you are to honor your wife as you would a special guest, love her unselfishly, love her as you love yourself, putting her needs first, no matter what!"

By putting up with your husband's selfishness, you are encouraging him to be indolent, and disobedient to God and His design for your marriage. Not only is he to put your needs first, but he is to provide for you.

Quit your job. If he gets hungry enough, he'll get one. Then, instead of staying home and resting all day so he can use you, he'll be the tired one and won't be so demanding. That will make it easier for you to submit to his desires. Meanwhile, have an understanding with him: For his good, you will not be available every night. You are going to help him control his demands so he will be in a better position to obey God.

One woman with a similar situation took us at our word. The next day after we counseled with her she gave notice on her job, told her husband and he said, "Well, I guess I'd better go get work." She was so excited, she found out where we were staying, dashed in, danced about and whirled me around, telling me all about it. "I just know things are going to get better!" she laughed.

Cure-All?

Men need understanding, too! For example:

> *My husband always wants sex shen he gets depressed. He says it will help him but it never does.*

Lovemaking should be an expression of joy, not a relief from depression. But, perhaps he's like the woman who gets sick so she won't HAVE to have sex. He gets sick so he CAN have it. If you have a little boy, you know how important it is to him to be cuddled and loved by his Momma. When he grows up, he's going to need a wife who will care for him, too. Maybe your husband is just crying for more attention from you and the knowledge that you really love him. If he gets depressed often, find out why. He may need professional help.

The Low Blow

Here is a wife who's using an old standby weapon:

> *My wife withholds sex as a punishment for getting her own way. What can I do about this?*

Keep close tabs the next few weeks on what she is demanding. You may see a pattern start to form which will show you where her needs lie. Then try to read between the lines. When a woman isn't getting the love and attention she needs from her husband, she will sometimes point those desires in another direction and start asking for favors, material things, or some other substitute. A man will use reverse tactics. When a woman "doesn't want to" he will punish her by pouting, becoming angry, threatening to find another woman or some other threat designed to bring her to bay. Either way, it is playing dirty pool. Your mate is a human being, not a puppy you're training. Change your tactics. You are driving a destructive wedge between you.

LOVEMAKING CAN BE UMMMMM

Why settle for less than the best, husband? You have entered the bedroom, or the living room, or are settling down in front of the fire with your wife, intending to make love. The choice is yours: Make this a memorable, joy-filled occasion for her (and for you) or let it be a ho-hum, here-we-go-again experience.

We are assuming that you have been very careful to do all sorts of nice things for your wife the last three days. You told her you loved her each day; and told her how lovely she was (twice); listened to her talk; brought her a little surprise (a daisy from the garden) and generally got her thinking you were the greatest!

Today, you stopped by the drugstore on the way home for a little gift (a pretty package of bubblebath?) which you are going to give her now.

You have already taken a bath and put on cologne and some attractive garments. You have squeezed two glasses of orange juice and poured it into your prettiest goblets. GOOD START!

Now you can do some or all of the following:

- turn on soft music
- brush her hair (if she likes it)
- tickle her back (if she likes it)
- kiss her gently—a lot
- hold her in your arms while you tell her something funny that happened today (nothing about other women)
- give her a butterfly kiss with your eyelashes
- sing her a love song
- tell her she's beautiful
- write messages with your finger in the palm of her hand or on her arm.

Etc., etc., etc.

Now, isn't that fun? And it'll make each time together so special she'll look forward to them.

How long you prepare her, when you get down to serious loveplay, depends on her. Ask her to tell you when she is ready for intercourse. If it takes her a half hour, then give her a half hour! Or longer. Or shorter. Be careful you don't reach a climax before she does.

The Ultimate

Is it always necessary for the woman to have an orgasm?

Is it necessary to drink anything but water? You don't ever have to have an orgasm. It's just that when you don't, it's like baking a pie and not being able to eat any of it. Both you and your husband always should strive for this goal. Be sure he is stimulating the clitoris properly and you should have no trouble. (For further information concerning the sexual organs, read the relevant books listed in our Bibliography.)

One bride asked for help in this area. A few months later, her letter came: "Thank you for your help. Everything is great now. Just great!"

Speak Up!

How can I approach my husband without embarrass-ing him and myself to let him know there should be more foreplay before physical love?

Tell him you're not ready. Men don't have a crystal ball they can gaze into which will say, "NOW!" It may embarrass you and him the first time around, but chances are it won't. Remember that when you and your husband consummated your marriage, you became ONE. Would you hesitate to deal with yourself on any matter? Give it a try. No one ever learned to swim by reading a book about it. Be loving and gentle in your tone of voice. Communication in this important area of your life together is essential.

What's the National Average?

> *How often should we make love? My desires are less than my husband's and I feel guilty about it.*

Why should you feel guilty? You might become more motivated if he romanced you on days when he isn't planning to make love. If you reduce your lovemaking to where you are counting the times or setting the day, you're heading into stormy waters. Sometimes you will want to make love just to please him, but the general rule is: Make love when you both have a desire. For some it is twice a week or once a week or more often. The important thing is quality—not quantity.

You Mean There's More Than One?

> *What type of sex is all right for married couples?* [*oral, etc.*]

The Bible says, "Marriage is honorable in all, and the bed undefiled: but whoremongers and adulterers God will judge." Some feel this means that anything goes as long as the couple is married. Not necessarily so.

When a questionable type of lovemaking comes up, you might ask yourself some questions: When I participate in this, do I feel guilty? Am I asking for help because I feel uneasy about it? Is one partner insisting while the other is reluctant? Is the answers are yes, then take a firm stand against it. If neither of you feel guilt or compunction, then it is between you and God.

INHIBITIONS AND LOW SEX DRIVE

Victoria Is Still Blowing Her Horn

> *My wife has a victorian idea of sex. It's caused her two nervous breakdowns.*

It may have added to the breakdowns, but there is doubt that it was the main cause. She may have some deep-seated fears from her childhood that may or may not be connected with sex, but have erupted in that way. She should have professional counseling. She also needs a husband who treats her very tenderly, romancing her at great length, with very few demands on her sexually until she becomes healthy. Make sure that when you do make love to her, it is a beautiful experience. Be thoughtful of her feelings.

> *My wife feels sex is dirty.*

Much of what is being fed the public today *is* dirty . . . jokes . . . pornography . . . suggestiveness . . . prostitution in the open. But sex, as God intended it, should be beautiful in the well-adjusted life. You will have to begin an education program. Start with reading the Song Of Solomon in the Bible. I did a detailed treatise of this lovely portrait of married love in *Forever My Love.*

> *The topic of S-E-X is not permitted in our house.*

Why not? If you have children, you are doing them a grave injustice. They will have to go to their friends at school for their information. They'll be sneaking looks at magazines, books and articles on the subject, trying to fill a legitimate need to know. If you have hang-ups, find out why, and correct them. The topic of sex should never be made a common thing, but it should be as natural to mention it in the home as any other normal function of life. If the children see you don't make a big thing of it, FOR or AGAINST, they'll grow up with healthy attitudes. Answer their questions simply and truthfully.

> *I'm bashful and worry whether what my husband and I do is right or wrong when we make love.*

Quit worrying. God started the whole business. If you have a sensitive conscience, that will guide you. Just enjoy each other.

The Reluctant Swain

Several women have asked us questions similar to this one:

> *My husband is not interested in sex. We engage in it once every two or three months. What can I do about it?*

Your husband might need counseling professionally. There has to be a reason and it could be one of the following:

- a childhood experience. Perhaps he never saw affection expressed between his parents, or he may have had something traumatic happen to him which he can't recall right now
- he may have a deficiency of male hormones
- he may be a homosexual or a transvestite
- he may be physically ill
- or mentally ill
- he may be having an affair

It may not be ANY OF THESE THINGS. It will be unhealthy for either of you to go on worrying about this. Find out, if he is willing. If he is not willing, then count your blessings. Many women would trade places with you any day, because they have become so disgusted with sex.

IT'S ALL WRONG

Homosexuality

In our newspaper last night was an interview with a well-known author who is proudly a homosexual. He has lived with his "lover" for twenty-four years. Some quick arithmetic painted the picture. His "lover" was a child of sixteen when he fell under this man's spell. The author is close to thirty years older. In California, homosexuality is encouraged by politicians who seek the votes of these people rather than stand against immorality. Although we generally don't have homosexuals or lesbians coming to our marriage seminars, for obvious reasons, we have dealt with some on an individual basis, like the following:

> *I am a married man with two children. I've left my wife and am living with another man. I used to be a lay preacher. I know my homosexuality is a sin, but I am powerless to do anything about it.*

Lesbianism

A woman reared in an orphanage where affection and love were not shown and whose mother never came to see her, asked this:

> *I used to engage in sexual acts with my roommate, but have quit since I became a Christian. She is the one who led me to find Christ. She says the Bible is against homosexuality, but there's nothing wrong with lesbianism. What do you think?*

God loves the homosexual. He also loves the lesbian. He loves the person who "changes" his or her sex. But He HATES their sin, and that's what it's all about. Herbert J. Miles writes in *Sexual Understanding Before Marriage*, ". . . the assumption that a homosexual has a compulsion, caused by society, over which he has no control, is to be rejected. Many others who have had the same strong drives and have grown up in the same society with similar family backgrounds have freely, yet firmly rejected temptations to homosexuality. The practicing homosexual is a sinner against God and man and in due process develops into a sick person. This is not meant to ignore the fact that personality development is influenced by environment. . ."[1]

Let's back him up with Scripture: "God therefore handed them over to disgraceful passions. Their women exchanged the normal practices of sexual intercourse for something which is abnormal and unnatural. Similarly the men, turning from natural intercourse with women, were swept into lustful passions for one another. Men with men performed these shameful horrors, receiving, of course, in their own personalities the consequences of sexual perversity. Moreover since they considered themselves too high and mighty to acknowledge God, He allowed them to become the slaves of their degenerate minds . . ."

We doubt that homosexuals and lesbians can ever find release from this sin that grips them except by the power of God. Therefore, if you are steeped in this sin, we recommend:

- surrender your life to Christ
- avoid your homosexual and lesbian friends totally, even if it means you have to change jobs or move
- get into strong Christian company (church, social groups)
- avoid close relationships with members of your own sex for whom you may have attraction

1. Herbert J. Miles, *Sexual Understanding Before Marriage*, Grand Rapids, Michigan. Zondervan, Publishing House, 1971.

- ask Christians who are concerned about you to pray for you (choose carefully)
- spend much time in God's Word and prayer
- avoid alcohol, it lowers your inhibitions
- go to a Christian psychologist or psychiatrist. He or she will be in sympathy with your intent to turn away from your problem

With God's help, the enemy will be defeated, if you mean business.

Then There's The Sadist

> My husband abuses me physically, including when we have sex. What should be my attitude toward this?

You might consider calling the police when he abuses you and have them arrest him. He is committing a crime.

Unfortunately there is little satisfaction in this area. Some reports claim that policemen avoid family mayhem because more of them are injured or killed trying to break up lovers' quarrels than in all other areas of law enforcement put together. That viewpoint is hooted down by scores of women who claim that the police don't try or aren't interested. They say that police will come to the door and walk away with nothing more than a word of warning to the husband. Others report that when they go to the police station for protection, they are treated shabbily and sent right home again, often to worse treatment.

If the police are unable or unwilling to protect you, then go to the City Hall or wherever criminal complaints are filed in your town. Sign a warrant for your husband's arrest.

Sometimes your best bet is an attorney. Every now and then, George gets a frantic call from a woman in this position. One night, I heard him say, "Have you any place to go where he can't find you?" She did. "Go there, now." She did. The next day, her respectable businessman husband was served at his office with a subpoena. He never touched his wife again. If you don't wish to do anything quite so drastic, separate from him until he changes his ways. (See further suggestions in Chapter 12, *Physical and Mental Abuse*.)

> *My husband has started making advances toward our teenage daughter. She says to me, "Don't ever leave me alone with that creep." He won't go for counseling. My son is making advances toward her too. What can I do?*

Your job at this time is to protect your daughter at all costs. Incest seems to be on the increase, as the morals of our country plummet. Have a frank talk with your daughter and see how she feels about a solution. It might be best to put her in a Christian home where the people are well adjusted until she is out of school and starts to form a life of her own. If so, see her daily, if possible. Have a frank talk with your son, pointing out the evils and dangers of incest. Explain to him that he is being affected by his father, who is in great need of professional counseling.

Old Fashioned! Who? Me?

When I was being interviewed on the TV talk show, AM San Francisco, a male caller said, among other things,

> *I believe you are old fashioned. A man should be allowed to have many partners, not just one. He'll be much happier that way.*

Who's old fashioned? What he proposes has been around since man first shook his fist in the face of God. When it all began, God said, "For this cause shall a man leave his father and mother and shall cleave to his wife; and they shall become one flesh." Later, He stated, ". . . A man shall leave his father and mother, and shall cleave to his wife; and the two shall become one flesh. Consequently they are no more two, but one flesh. What therefore God has joined together, let no man separate."

Furthermore, we're told, concerning sexual sin: "To avoid fornication, let every man have his own wife and let every woman have her own husband." Throughout the Bible, God holds up the marriage relationship between a husband and wife as the right way. He commanded man to supply his wife's emotional needs by loving her as his own flesh. No woman can bear the idea of sharing her man with another woman. Any man who spreads his favors is certainly not loving his wife. And I ask you, "If you truly loved a woman, would you want to be just one of many men in her life?" Or have you ever had the experience of truly loving?

Solomon had seven hundred wives and three hundred concubines and they were his downfall, despite all his wisdom. David was a man after God's own heart, but it was because he loved God and put his trust in Him that God honored him despite his multiplicity where women were concerned. And at last, his defiance of one of God's laws, "Thou shalt not commit adultery," got him in serious trouble and made a murderer of him as he comforted himself with Bathsheba.

P.S. from George: There's a solution to every bedroom problem if you look in the right place and are willing to accept what will help. The time to start is *now*.

4

Communication—
The Key To Riches

THERE'S A WALL BETWEEN US

Numbers of women, and some men, have made the complaint that their mates just won't talk to them. Nations go to war because leaders can't communicate. Husbands and wives go to divorce courts. George tells of two sisters who lived in the same house and hadn't spoken to each other for thirty years! Fearful or angry people shut themselves up in their caves, refusing to come out or let anyone else in. I don't know why you've holed up away from the ones who love you, but we might take a look at some maybe's.

MAYBE:

- you are deeply angry at someone. Your mother? Your father? God? (Whomever, perhaps your mate touched off the firecracker by a series of negatives he or she tossed your way) . . .
- you grew up in a home where they didn't talk . . .
- your mate is a strong, overbearing personality and you feel defeated . . .
- you don't want anyone invading your private world where you are king or queen . . .

- you always end up wrong in a discussion so don't want to risk it anymore . . .
- you are immature and don't want to accept responsibility of supplying another's needs . . .
- you enjoy making others suffer . . .
- you are punishing your mate . . .
- you are feeling sorry for yourself . . .

or something else.

Mike is mad at God. You know why? One of his children was born mentally retarded. His other children, all healthy and normal, are growing up without a father's love because of his anger. His wife has no one with whom she can share because he won't talk with her. Kinda dumb, isn't it?

There is no problem that can't be solved, if you bring it out in the light so you can quit fumbling in the dark. If you can't do it on your own, we would like to make a couple of suggestions:

1. Get professional help. Be sure you don't get a counselor who has as many hang-ups as you. We suggest highly qualified, well-recommended Christian counselors.

And a sure-fire solution is to—

2. Turn to the Master Healer of hurts, the Lord Jesus Christ. A surrender of your life and any sin to Him will move you out of the darkness! He's just a prayer away. When God heals, He does it right and it lasts.

King Or Jester

Here's a king who has retreated to his castle:

I have been married twenty-five years. My husband has moved to his own room, keeps our bank accounts without my name on them, never apologizes for anything and never has. Although I have developed my own career and am being blessed and living closer to Jesus everyday, I would like to see my husband change. What do you suggest?

Get's pretty sticky, doesn't it? But even though this husband is a tortured human being, *you* don't have to be.

- Search your heart. Discover everything in your life that has aided in the deterioration of your marriage. It's important you don't make excuses like, "But I did it because he . . ." Your responsibility is to look at your shortcomings, not his.
- Determine, with God's help, to change personality traits, habits or anything in you that might be an irritant to your husband.
- Determine to think no negative thoughts about him, from now on. Only positive ones.
- Have a talk with him. Rehearse the mistakes you have made and share them with him, apologizing sincerely for making his life miserable. If he won't listen, write him a letter.
- Start thanking God that He is going to continue helping you become a lovelier person. Pray continually for your husband and exhibit only sweet, loving kindness to him, no matter how he has hurt you in the past.

He may start thawing. But even if he doesn't, you will be happier and more at peace.

Either Way I'm Wrong

Maybe this sounds familiar to you:

> *I don't speak back or disagree with him, because it makes him angry. But when I keep quiet, he takes that as meaning I am disagreeing with him and he still gets angry. Should I continue to keep quiet?*

Hard fellow to please, isn't he? Maybe you could get used to using such phrases as, "What you say certainly has merit. I'll have to think about it," or "You do have a point there. I'll think about it for awhile," or "I'm not sure what I think about it yet. I'll try to see it from your viewpoint." Avoid conflict as much as possible. If you have material which you feel would help him, approach him with the request that he read it to give you his thoughts on it because "you have a lot of perception." Don't be untruthful, but realize that most people do have some good ideas about most things.

The Clam

> How can I get him to open up and give me his opinion? How can I get him to share his personal feelings?

Ask yourself these questions:

- Do I usually give my opinion before he has a chance?
- When he has given his opinion, have I tended to disagree with him often?
- Do I hammer at him to get him to talk?
- When he has disagreed with me, have I gone ahead and done it my way?

If you have answered yes to any of these you may have the reason for his silence. Maybe you just talk too much and he doesn't want to make it worse by joining in. Tone yourself down. Speak only of important or interesting things. Keep chitchat at a minimum. Talk more about the positive than the negative. Maybe he'll come out of his shell and talk *with* you. If he does share something, don't scare him off with too many prying questions or over-eagerness.

I Was Carefully Taught

Here's the other side of the picture:

A man says: *My family never talked much. When I needed to know things or share, I went to my friend's homes and talked with their parents instead. I know I need to change, but how can I?*

A wife says: *I was taught as a child not to talk or show emotions. This has caused trouble in our marriage. What can I do?*

Rehearse when you are alone. Standing in front of a mirror, experiment. Think of something happy and laugh. Think of something sad and show sorrow in your face. Say something about different situations aloud, as if you were talking to someone else. Take acting lessons. It would help to be in a few plays even if you perform only walk-on parts. When in public, force yourself to smile at people (even when *they* aren't smiling), or to say something (to a clerk, a bagboy, the service station attendant). Tell your wife or husband what you are trying to do. Force yourself to respond for her or his sake and you'll see people react favorably. You'll soon be enjoying life!

What about lying? If I don't feel nice things about my wife in my heart, how can I say them?

Oh, come on now! There must be SOMETHING nice about your wife that you can express sincerely. Maybe you are being a super-critical person. It's time to change, get off the negative, accentuate the positive and reach out to make her feel like the beautiful, lovely person she can be, with your help.

COMMUNICATION BUILDER

Remember this little gem that has been paraphrased many different ways since it first appeared in 1828?

All the world is wrong but me and thee,
And lately I've begun to wonder about thee.

What we need to do is stand squarely in front of a mirror,

level a finger right at the old face and say, "You're no prize either, you fathead."

Sure your mate has wronged you, over and over again. Now it's time to dig a hole, bury the past and cover it up with an impenetrable lid. Some people figure it's easier if they don't say ANYthing, but that's just hiding in the bushes. Communication isn't really all that hard.

One of the biggest hindrances to understanding another person is allowing preconceived ideas to color our thinking. Such ideas are not so affectionately referred to as male chauvinism or female inconsistency. For instance:

IN THE MALE MIND

When The Husband	*When His Wife*
• gives his opinion, he is setting things straight.	• disagrees with him, she is challenging his leadership.
• talks on the telephone, it's an important call	• talks on the telephone, she is wasting time.
• asks the wife firmly to do something, he is showing leadership.	• asks him firmly to do something, she is being officious.
• repeats a request more than once, he is patiently reminding her.	• repeats a request more than once, she is nagging.
• is late to an appointment with his wife, he has a good excuse.	• is late to their meeting, she *has* no excuse.
• is late to dinner, he was busy.	• is late cooking dinner, she is inefficient.

- buys something, it's because it is essential.

- makes a mistake on their bank account, he feels it's no big thing.

- is sick, he deserves moment by moment attention and sympathy.

- doesn't want to make love, he has good reasons.

- reads while she tries to discuss something, he can do two things at once.

- does something stupid, he feels it is an honest mistake.

- has extra-curricular activities, he needs to realize his dreams.

- works at the church, he is doing the Lord's work.

- makes a purchase, she's spending him into bankruptcy.

- makes a mistake on their bank account, she is stupid and is going to land them both in jail one of these days.

- is sick, she is expected to be up and at 'em by the second day.

- wants to wait until another time, she is just trying to get out of it.

- reads while he is talking to her, she doesn't care about his things.

- does something stupid, she should laugh when he says, "If you had a brain, you'd be dangerous."

- wants to use her talents, she belongs in the kitchen.

- works at the church, she should be home taking care of him.

Like mother-in-law jokes, this kind of thinking leaves a woman feeling limp like the dishrag she soon will learn to hate.

But she's no paragon of virtue in this field either. Take a look at what's going on in HER MIND!

IN THE FEMALE MIND

When She	*When He*
• says, "It's time you did a little disciplining around here," she's helping him take his position as head of the family.	• does as she asks, she has a right to butt in and criticize.
• puts time saving techniques to work around the house, she is clever.	• suggests time saving ideas, he is interfering with her schedule.
• doesn't keep a promise, it's because she has a right to change her mind.	• doesn't keep his promise, he is a rat.
• can't get a point across during an argument, she has a right to cry.	• can't get a point across during an argument, he is a beast if he gets angry.
• wants to watch TV, she needs the relaxation.	• watches TV, he is ignoring her.
• doesn't want to join him in a favorite recreation, she is exerting her right to be an individual.	• doesn't want to join her in her activities he is being inconsiderate.
• blows it and her husband says, "I told you so," he is picking on her.	• blows it and she says, "I told you so," she is just helping him for the future.
• laughs at her husband's mistakes, she is being cute.	• laughs at her mistakes, he is insensitive.

- stays up too late, she has things she has to do.

- criticizes her husband's outfit, she is making him a fashionplate.

- criticizes a dish she has cooked, she is being mature and honest with herself.

- comments about how good looking someone of the opposite sex is, she is being observant.

- criticizes, she intends it constructively.

- stays up too late, he doesn't care about his health.

- criticizes her outfit, he thinks she looks ugly.

- does the same, he thinks she's an awful cook.

- comments about the cute secretary, he is comparing her with his wife.

- criticizes, he does it to be mean.

In our seminars, we send couples off into workshops together. One of our sessions is all about POSITIVE talking back and forth. Let's try it. If the one you once loved so madly (and can again) will do it at the same time, it will be best. If not, try the following alone.

FIRST MONTH:
Step 1   List all the things on paper that you LIKE about your mate.
Step 2   Every day, for the next month, compliment your mate with one of the items on the list. FOR EACH COMPLIMENT YOU GIVE, AWARD YOURSELF *10 POINTS!*
(Example: "I think your hair is lovely," or
"I like the way your eyes twinkle.")
If you add "I love you" or another endearing term you aren't used to using, GIVE YOURSELF AN

ADDITIONAL *10 POINTS*.
(NO-NO: Sarcasm is forbidden. Dish out with sincerity.)

Step 3   At the end of the month, check your score.
Excellent - 300
Good   - 240
Average - 150 (Dullsville)
Poor   - let's not talk about it.

SECOND MONTH:

Step 1   Continue the daily compliments. Make a list of things you LIKE about *yourself* to keep on hand when spirits droop.

Step 2   Make a list of things you DO NOT LIKE about yourself, including things you do that aggravate the trouble at home.
(One fellow wouldn't write anything down on the don't likes. He wasn't kidding anyone. His list should have started in the bedroom, gone through the kitchen and circled the yard twice.)

Step 3   Now, the challenging part! You're going to share one of the *don't likes* on your list with your mate. By getting your faults in the open with the one who is already irritating you by telling you about them, you can cut through your own *pride*. The resulting humility provides a fertile ground for improvement.

Tell your mate what you plan to do to correct your fault.
(Example: A. State problem. "I worry about things too much."
B. State solution. "I'm going to try to trust God in my life more. I'm going to keep my mind filled with good thoughts so worry won't have a chance to dwell there. And, I'm

going to listen to tapes by speakers
and read books on positive thinking.

C. Start correcting your faults.

EACH TIME YOU MAKE A CON-
SCIOUS EFFORT AND *SUCCEED*
GIVE YOURSELF *20 POINTS*.

Step 4   Continue working on that weakness.
Continue complimenting your mate.

Step 5   At end of month, check your score (including
compliments and sweet nothings)

Excellent - 600
Good   - 400
Average - 250 (Dullsville)
Poor   - let's not talk about it.

(NO-NO: If your mate taunts you about your
failures, prick his or her balloon by
simply agreeing and saying, "I'm sorry.
I'll try harder." No cutting remarks
from you. He or she will begin to feel *so*
guilty.

During this period, no criticizing of
mate. If you feel you simply HAVE to,
couple it with a compliment, like:
"Honey, please don't growl at me.
You're too pretty for that," or "You
didn't get done what I asked? (count to
10) Well, you must have had a good
reason [smile]."

FOR EACH CRITICISM OF MATE, SUBTRACT *20
POINTS*.

FOURTH MONTH:

Keep complimenting
Keep working on old faults
Choose new fault and deal with it

Continue the program through a 12-month period. If you fall splat on your face in the mud, pick yourself up, jump over the ditch and keep going!

Because you are learning to GIVE; because you are learning to ENCOURAGE; because you are learning to look at yourself honestly and do something about your weaknesses, by the end of the year, even though you won't be a total conqueror, you will be a new person, ready to reach new heights in the following year. And very likely, you will discover a miraculous change in your mate as well.

Now, isn't that better than bickering or non-communication?

TALKING IT OVER

Getting Personal

> *How do you and George settle a debate between you when you each have your own ideas on how it should be decided, or are you so in tune with each other that you have no debates?*

Two strong personalities like us not having debates? No way. We have learned, however, to talk things over without getting uptight (most of the time).

When we were newly married, and I was angry or my feelings were hurt, I sometimes refused to talk. George always did one of two things: He would say, "Honey, we can't settle this thing if we don't talk about it. Come on now," or "I'm terribly sorry, dear. I shouldn't have done that to you." It always melted me like ice cream left in the sunshine. Who can stay mad after THAT? Then we could both talk it over sensibly without heat. I was more willing to admit by then that he might be right and he could better see my viewpoint.

When you are able to talk peacefully, listen patiently to each other without interrupting.

If you still disagree on an issue, then the husband must make the decision. This puts a big responsibility on his shoulders, of course, for he is to love his wife as he loves himself, and therefore must make the decision for her good, rather than for his own. See Chapter 7, *Who's Running This Show Anyway?*

A Cautious Husband

When is the best time to bring up sticky questions concerning family problems with my wife?

When you aren't tired, rushed or distracted with the children. Don't choose the week before her menstrual period if it's possible to avoid it, or whenever her tensions are greatest. Select a time when you aren't angry or irritated. All discussions should be frank, but kindly so.

Wouldn't it be nice, though, if she were mature enough so that you didn't have to worry about when or where and how? Oh, well . . . .

The Know It Alls

How do you get a wife to hear what you want to say when she already starts answering the question before you ask it?

Patiently listen and wait for her to finish. Then tell her that you wish to comment now without interruption because you listened to her without breaking in. If she interrupts, remind her firmly that it is now your turn. She can speak after you have finished.

My wife always has a patronizing attitude when we talk. She just won't listen to me.

Analyze the way you discuss things. Do you get heated? Do you press your lips in a thin line and set your jaw? If so, learn a soft, patient "you-always-have-good-ideas" attitude, putting your ideas forth in between hers, if possible. If you do that already, and she still looks down her nose at you, you have an immature wife who has not learned to honor or respect her husband (nor anyone else, probably). Just love her into listening to you. For instance: "Now, honey, I may not have the same ideas as you, but I want you to listen to my viewpoint, and maybe you'll see that what I suggest has merit." Then, after hearing hers, if you are still convinced you are right, go ahead and make decisions accordingly. It's hard to break down immature attitudes in patronizing people, and you'll have to go at it gradually.

Tune Her Down

Here's a fellow who married a vibrating, scintillating personality and now he's complaining about it.

My wife comes on too strong. It turns me off.

Well, quit turning off. Just let her bluster about a bit. Her strength is probably one of the things that attracted you to her in the first place. If it takes an unpleasant tack sometimes, so what? After she booms it out, then, with a twinkle in your eye and a loving hug, say "Explain it to me again, dear, quietly and logically and I'll consider it." Be fair. Consider both sides before you make any decisions.

She Thinks - He Thinks

Some men are willing but confused:

> *I know our problem is because I can't understand her viewpoint, and I don't give consideration to what she thinks. I'm stuck. What now?*

At least you are honest and have analyzed the situation. The next time an issue comes up, try having her write her viewpoint out for you, so you can think it over in private. (It could be she is talking so much you are confused, or she doesn't express herself well.) As you read her viewpoint, write down any questions you have that will make it clearer to you. Talk over your suggestions with her, but if it gets confusing again, have her write her answers to your questions, and then retreat again to figure them out.

Maybe This Came From His Wife

> *My husband is a wonderful, kind man, but as far as he is concerned, what has happened to me everyday, joys or sorrows are not important. I have gotten to where I don't share things with him, because he doesn't try to understand me as a person. How can I get him to change?*

Women need to talk—about little things—about big things. They prefer sharing with the one who is closest to them, their husbands. If you have explained to your husband how important it is to you to have his interest and he still refuses to listen, then adjust your desires. Instead, encourage him to talk about *his* day. Be genuinely interested. Be thankful you have a "wonderful, kind man." Many can't say that!

HOW HONEST SHOULD I BE?

Before you are honest about anything, you ought to take a good look at our Communication Builder in this chapter.

It's so EASY to see the other person's faults and be so sure that we need to set them straight. But many, many traits will correct themselves when you start delighting your mate with more loving attentions, appreciating the good things he or she does aloud and building them up verbally.

If, however, you have been very generous with your praises and you feel there's no other way for things to change, then speak your piece honestly and kindly.

Even then, use the positive approach. Here's a fellow who feels it's time:

> *How frank should a husband be with his wife in shar-ing a problem that he knows may hurt her, but he feels it is hindering their relationship?*

Ask her to tell you the things *you* are doing that bother *her*. Write them down as she talks. Tell her you will do everything you can to improve in those areas (and start as soon as your talk is over). Then tell her you love her very much but there is something that is bothering you which you feel you must share with her. When she realizes that you care how SHE feels about the things you do that bother *her*, she'll be more than willing to listen to what *she's* doing wrong, and to respond in positive ways.

Make It Plain

More than one woman has asked:

> *Is it fair to underline what you think is applicable in your books for my husband? He tends to skip over the important things, not realizing that they apply to him.*

If he is a reasonable man, why not? It would be much easier for him to take it from a book than from you verbally. Many men have shared with us that their wives did just exactly that. In every case, the marriage began to improve. Your husband may not honestly know he is doing certain things that upset you, and may be grateful to you for pointing them out.

We're Slipping

How do you make the marriage work if you don't know how and you've started to lose respect? I still love my spouse very much but not like I used to. I want to regain what we had in the beginning but he doesn't want to work at it. He thinks there is nothing wrong, I guess.

This young man is ignoring danger signals. Men like this need someone to frankly point out to them that they are heading for the cliff and, if they don't change direction, they'll go over it. Get him to read our books. If he won't, read them *to* him. Then have a frank talk with him, explaining your feelings in the critical areas.

Don't Be A Blabbermouth

How honest and truthful and open should a husband and wife be in relating past pre-marriage experiences?

You should always be honest and truthful with your mate. That doesn't mean you have to tell everything you know. Share what you must to answer direct questions and leave unsaid the things that would cause unhappiness, unless your silence would bring about suspicion and fear that would be greater than if the person knew the details. In most cases, questions concerning the past are better never asked.

Disdain With A Capital "D"

How can you say nice things to your mate when you feel she is unbearable or has done something which particularly bugs you?

Oh, come on now! "Unbearable" is a strong word. Take a look inside yourself to see what you might be doing that is causing her to be unbearable or to bug you. Are you supplying her emotional needs? A woman will become a delight to her husband once he catches on to this approach. But a woman who is under constant criticism or condemnation will blunder and make mistakes far more than one who isn't.

Walking On Eggshells

How do I get my husband to accept things in marriage without feeling manipulated or smothered?

He needs to understand that being head of the wife doesn't give him dictator's rights. You are his helpmeet to help him meet the challenges of life. How can you help him if he's the only one who dares to express an opinion?

How do I go about dealing with a complaining husband. He complains about the weather, his aches and pains, etc. But not about me!

Be thankful he doesn't complain about you! Maybe *he* needs more loving, romantic attention! Compliment him frequently! When it rains, say "Oh, what a blessing! It's raining! Just think how terrible it would be if we had a drought!" He may have a lot of aches and pains that are signaling that serious health trouble lies ahead. Better check them out.

QUARRELING AND MAKING UP

Nations quarrel. Neighbors quarrel. Everybody's quarreling, including our cats and dogs. Why? We're egocentric people, that's why. We're concerned about NUMBER ONE, that's why. We're battling an unseen enemy, that's why. When you stop to really think about it, quarreling should be so ridiculous to us that we wouldn't even consider it.

A woman who attends our church told me once, "My husband and I have never had a quarrel." I didn't want to doubt her word, but it was so unusual that my eyes bugged out and I said, "Never?" And, like the captain in the musical sings, she said, "No, never!" She continued, "Paul is so even-tempered and low key, he just won't quarrel." I believed her. He is a wondrously mild-mannered man, and yet quietly a leader in the church. His wife is absolutely lovely, inside and out, and never looks as if she has a worry in the world.

How often we've heard people say, "If you didn't quarrel, marriage would be so dull," or "It's so much fun to make up." I've decided that's just rationalization at its best. We can't help ourselves, so we give excuses for doing the wrong thing. Quarreling isn't fun in anyone's book and there's a terrific amount of pain and stress involved before making up takes place.

Whose Move?

Quarrels are a reality, however, so we must deal with them.

When there is a serious quarrel between you, what steps do you take to end it or to arrive at a reconciliation?

You take the first step right over to your mate, swallow your pride and say, "Darling, I'm sorry for what I've done to cause us to quarrel. I feel you must have good reason for saying what you did. Forgive me for being unkind in my attitude." That's maturity.

Pride?

One sincere husband asks:

Why is it hard to get an answer to "What are you thinking?" during or after a conflict?

Another states:

She refuses to talk during a fight, so we can work it out. So I get stubborn.

So someone is refusing an all out battle? Great! Stop the fight. Gulp down your pride. Put your arms around her gently and say, "I'm sorry." Then kiss her tenderly (if she'll allow you). Add, "Let's talk about this when our emotions aren't so high."

Rude Dude

What is a woman to do when her husband tells her straight out to "grow up?"

Men tend to think a woman is being childish if she doesn't use his no-nonsense approach to discussions and shows emotion over things that are bothering her. The best way to fix his wagon is to quit being emotional when you talk. Don't discuss problems when you are tired, tense, or angry.

When he criticizes you, instead of getting upset, listen carefully, smile and say, "Thank you for pointing that out to me. I'll consider that." You know, he might just be saying something you need to hear.

Does the husband ever have the right to tell his wife to "shut up!" How should she respond to this?

When you and he have cooled down, quietly talk to him about this. You aren't dirt under his feet, and you don't want to be treated that way.

But before you do, be honest with your own life. Are you a woman who shouts, nags or gets ugly when you talk with him? If so, turn around and go the other direction and maybe you won't have to straighten him out.

P.S. from Margaret: Does someone you know feel you have wronged him or her? Make it right before night falls. Things left on the burner to cook overtime can start a fire!

5

Money! Money! Money!

THERE'S NEVER ENOUGH!

The fellow who edited one of my radio programs on which I interviewed a friend laughed when he came to one portion. He explained, "When she says things like 'Throw a load of clothes in the dryer' and 'out on the patio' I don't think she realizes that a lot of us don't have dryers and patios."

Maybe you DON'T have some of the items that others take for granted as necessities. But it has been obvious to us that many people distort the picture in their minds. Consequently they fall into habits that make others around them feel uncomfortable. If you are one who is struggling, consider these suggestions:

A) Be realistic: Are you sure you *never* have enough, or are you comparing yourself to others who have more? If so, your standards are not correct. One couple complains long and loud about never having as much as their friends, and yet they live in a far nicer apartment than many people we know. Some of their furniture is top grade. And they make a habit of doing things that we don't feel *we* can afford (like going to expensive concerts frequently or eating out once a week). They have fallen into the trap of trying to keep up with the faster pace the guy on the hill is setting.

If this is one of your problems, keep in mind that you have no idea what's really going on behind the neighbor's closed doors. One young, enthusiastic fellow we know set himself up in business and impressed everyone he met far and near with the gold fixtures he had in his luxurious home, the limousine equipped with telephone and the airplane he used to transport "clients" to and from Acapulco for nights of entertainment. Many a struggling couple looked at him with envy. The fact of the matter is he had a very big imagination supported by a gift of gab, but a very small bank account. Soon he was bankrupt.

Others are living totally on someone else's money, constantly in debt and very likely to stay that way most of their lives. There are more important things than striving for material goods that force you to live beyond your means.

Poor? Or Just A Big Mouth?

B) Besides being realistic, be careful you don't fall in the habit of "poor-mouthing" it. There is a pride that is good. It's synonymous with greatness, holding your head up high and walking like a child of God. Your friends, neighbors and relatives shouldn't know your financial status, unless one of them is helping you specifically.

If you think you are "poor," keep it your secret. Always avoid such phrases as:

"I wish we could afford things like that."
"I buy my clothes at a secondhand place."
"We can't afford it."
"We're so poor."
"Everyone is better off than we are."
"It's going to cost us . . ."

These wear thin in a hurry, give others a negative feeling about you, make you the subject of gossip and may embarrass your family.

Sharing The Wealth

C) No one likes a sponger. When you go to anyone's house to visit or to eat dinner (unless you visit back and forth all the time), take something, if nothing more than a little box of nuts. We have one friend who has had so many misfortunes, and continues to have them, that they would fill two pages in this book. But whenever we are able to have her and her children over, she never comes empty-handed, even though she is desperately in need. That's admirable.

On extended visits, if friends or relatives vacation with you as much as you do with them, then there is no need to help buy food when you head their way. But if you are the usual visitor and they are not, and you stay several days, no matter how "poor" you are and how "rich" they are (even if it's Mom and Pop), go shopping with them, plop down $25 or more when they pass the cash register and say, "I want to share in this. It will make me feel so much better." And if it doesn't make you feel better, it should. If they insist that you don't, then send a gift to them as soon as you get home, with a big thank you.

If you're saying, "Sure, that's easy for an attorney's wife to say," let me assure you, I've been there. When I was a kid, I would have had to wear flour sacks, I think, if my Aunt Winnie hadn't passed my cousin's clothes along to me. I doubt if Auntie knew what a valuable service she was performing since we were discouraged from sharing our financial burdens with anyone. Despite our position economically, it would have been considered embarrassing and cheap to take from others without returning in kind.

Fat Man - Skinny Man

In every family there seems to be one who takes things very seriously and one who does not. Like this:

> My wife never worries about money. She just thinks that everything will be there without our having to work towards it.

Although you must be careful how you spend, be glad there aren't two of you who stumble around with a mental money-bag on your shoulders, weighing you down. Borrow a little laughter from her and be careful you don't dwell on problems that haven't come up yet.

Some Apples Have Worms In Them

> My wife is always telling me to ask for more money from my boss, but she won't help me save any.

We counseled personally with this man and found out that he and his wife didn't communicate well on anything, and she was bored with sex. Money problems were only an indication of deeper difficulties. He needs to start all over again, hearkening back to the dating days. This will help them grow closer together; she will be more willing to do without the extra money and help him in the saving end of it. She's fighting him now because she is resentful.

The Poor Provider

> If your husband is not doing his job of providing for you and your family financially or otherwise, should you speak out, and if so, how strongly?

It depends on how mature your husband is as to how strongly

you tell him what you feel is important. Be sure you aren't wanting more than he is equipped to deliver. To expect a person who is perfectly suited to deliver mail to become a doctor could make for an unhappy husband and thus an unhappy home. Accept him for what he is. If you are sure he has greater potential, encourage him to develop it.

Many people fail to live up to their potential. A man often will get started in a job in order to make ends meet and never advance, because it's just too much effort to learn new skills and get more education.

BUDGETING AND CUTTING COSTS

My husband and I come from very different backgrounds. Mine was well to do. His was middle class. When we married, I bought what I wanted when I wanted it, charging things even though we didn't have the money. Now we are always paying minimum monthly bills for charges. How do we get out of debt? I've locked up the charge cards and don't use them except for absolute necessities.

Let's start with a true story. Shortly after Jerry married Darlene, he suffered a heart attack and they went immediately into debt. Darlene was pregnant with her first child and before the next year was out, she was pregnant with another. Since worry over their situation was making Jerry's condition worse, she took over with a determination to get out of debt and accomplish some definite goals. Those goals were:

1. Buy a car.
2. Pay off medical bills, including those incurred from the birth of their children.
3. Buy a house.
4. Buy necessary items for house (furniture, appliances, carpet, etc.)

5. Keep her children dressed adequately.

Although she wisely felt that being a full-time mother was more important than holding down a paying job, since her husband was still able to work, she did begin to baby-sit in their neighborhood in the evenings to supplement their income. He would be at home watching the children on those nights. She also did some mending and odd jobs, such as addressing Christmas cards for businessmen. She budgeted their income so that each month their doctors would receive a set amount on their bills. When they had to have clothes, she bought inexpensive and bargain clothes of good quality.

They bought a secondhand car and began payments on it.

They ate low-cost but nutritious foods, opting for beans and hamburger as well as casseroles, leaving steaks and expensive cuts for the future.

Darlene put a small amount of money towards a home in an "untouchable" bank account each month before any other spending was done. Gradually, the down payment fund grew big enough. They began looking for a house. They chose one that was a bit higher in cost because it was in a neighborhood that would go up in value rather than down. (Later that property doubled in price).

They moved all their old furniture from the apartment into the house and chose, as their first two purchases, a stove and a refrigerator.

By now the car was theirs, and they invested in a washing machine to cut down coin-machine and gas costs. She held off getting a vacuum cleaner, waiting until the day they could save enough cash for a carpet. It was harder work using a broom but it saved money. Eventually, they bought a dryer, and a T.V.

After the appliances were paid for, they started investing in some new furniture, starting with the living room. The time came when they were solvent—not rich—but solvent. I never saw their children looking shabby, their house dirty or unkempt, and they never went on welfare or begged for help.

It is important to note that they set goals; they didn't let the mountain they had to climb scare them off or depress them; they avoided luxuries altogether, taking their fun in little things, like family walks and games; they kept a positive, loving attitude toward each other throughout, with all members willing to make necessary sacrifices. It took several years, but they made it.

A couple asks:

> *We have tried to cut costs. But we don't see where we can trim any further.*

There are always ways. But do be sensible. For instance, to run down to get day-old bread is foolish. First, you spend more money on gas than you save and secondly, you sacrifice your family's health which brings about more doctor bills. But you *can* save money in the food area. The trick is to pay less but keep nutrition HIGH.

MEATS: If you can buy quantity for your freezer (should you have one) fine, but leave the quarter or half-beef buying for the future when your head is above water, unless you can get it as cheaply as the least expensive meats on sale. Steaks and expensive meats can wait. Super lean ground meat can be cooked in dozens of different ways.

SOUPS: Make all kinds. Nutritious, delicious! They'll save you cooking time too, because they'll last two days. Dried beans and vegetables with ham hocks or other meat add important proteins.

CASSEROLES: Cheese and milk with vegetables are a good meat substitute. Beans with hamburger go well together. Don't overlook soybeans.

AVOID:
- White flour (the nutritious part, the germ of the wheat, has been thrown to the hogs. Most of what you get is starch). Use whole wheat *pastry* flour for your baking. It's just as light and fluffy as your old "enriched" standby, and can be used with the same recipes. Health food stores carry it. Use whole grain breads.
- White rice, macaroni or similar products (get all vitamin brown rice and vegetable macaronis).
- Sugar (bad for teeth, brain, organs and behavior). Substitute honey, molasses or sugar that has mineral salts left in it. Even then, learn to do with less sweetening.
- Potato chips and other high cost extras. Make your own or wait.
- Canned foods—expensive and low in nutrition. High heat destroys vitamins. Home-canned is better, but second best to fresh foods.
- Frozen foods—expensive unless you grow your own or buy produce when price is low and freeze it yourself.
- Anything with preservatives or chemicals in it.

TRY:
- Raw vegetables as much as possible. One doctor told us that half of all meals eaten should be raw for higher vitamin and mineral intake. Otherwise, steam so that vitamins aren't thrown away with the cooking water. Undercook slightly.
- Wheat germ and powdered skim milk. Inexpensive, and they can be added to your pancakes or biscuit recipes for additional vitamins, minerals and protein.

IF AT ALL
POSSIBLE:

Grow a garden. There are big savings here if you plant surefire producers like: swiss chard, beans (fresh—and some to dry for soups), tomatoes and squashes. Even if you have nothing but a window box, it will save you money.

ENTER-
TAINMENT:

Romance is essential to a marriage, but it need not be expensive. My friend, Suzy, is a master at creating inexpensive *fun*. Among her ideas:

- a special night out on the patio. The children are not invited. They are to go to bed early or retire to their rooms. Husband and wife eat and dream under the stars.
- walks after dinner, or a quick run down to a nearby park or beach for an hour.
- games while munching things (evenings when children are otherwise occupied). Other evenings WITH children.
- a special reading and snacking time in bed.
- candlelight dinner on the floor for everyone.
- making scrapbooks together.
- working on stamp collections.

With a little imagination, you can think of dozens of things.

TRANSPOR-
TATION:

Car pool or bus at least half the time. Cars are expensive. Walk when you can. Some men ride bicycles to public transportation.

WHEN
BUYING
APPLIANCES:

Look for sales, but don't get cheap grade. Pay more and in the long run you'll pay less in repair bills and replacement.

WHEN BUYING CLOTHES:	The same thing goes. Good quality will last. Poor quality costs. Buy infrequently, mix and match outfits, both men and women, so you can make those pieces stretch. Start with a good basic outfit that you'll have to budget into your plans. It will be fairly expensive. Slowly but gradually, build around that outfit, so you will have 3 or 4 in one.

- Save ahead so you can buy shoes and other clothes after Christmas while good sales are on.
- If you sew well, make your own wardrobe. A sewing machine for a good seamstress is a necessary investment.

GIFT WRAPPING:	Use tissue or buy your other wrapping after Christmas during sales.
CHRISTMAS CARDS:	We know many young couples who make their own.
CHRISTMAS PRESENTS:	Your loved ones should be remembered, but the gifts needn't be expensive. Many people make theirs. I recall through the years, since I was tiny, how my sister, Natalie, handled it. Wherever she was in the world (for some years she had to struggle financially) she never failed to send a present to all of us at Christmas and on birthdays. They always arrived on time and they were always a delight to open because she invariably chose something "different," or "unusual," though inexpensive. It took her time to find them and a sharp eye, but she was rewarded and so were we.

TOYS:

Why do your children have to have all the latest, expensive toys? We know one couple who were and are very wealthy. Despite that, they have always kept their Christmas and birthday gifts simple and at a minimum. If the children wanted big things like bicycles, they had to earn money for them themselves. We did the same with ours. Children learn thrift, a desire to work and appreciation for what they do receive.

Teaching your children that they have to have as much as Jimmy down the street is setting them up for the very trap from which you are trying to extricate yourself.

BABIES:

If you are a young couple, plan your family. It costs money, and lots of it, to have a baby these days.

PETS:

We all love them, but very often the people who have the least insist on the most. We've known families with 5 dogs and 6 cats whose children look like refugees. Animals are expensive, not only in terms of food, but in wear and tear on a place.

WISE INVESTMENTS

"Go for broke" is the philosophy of some, when it comes to investing, and they often do just that, go broke. Others seem to press the magic button every time. One friend called George and said, "Guess what? I invested some money in an oil well a few weeks ago and it gushed up $200,000 for me!" A few weeks before, he had bought a huge hunk of land that has since doubled in price. Most of us don't know the right people or have the know-how to find gushing oil wells and strike-it-rich land to supplement our incomes. But wise investing is within everyone's reach, even if it is on a modest level.

What About Buying A Home?

One man wrote:

> *I believe we should buy everything for cash. My wife wants to buy a home. But I say "rent" until we have the cash.*

My husband taught me almost everything I know about economics and there's still a lot I haven't taken the time to get through my head. But some gems ring loud and clear. One of them is: A home is one of the best investments a person can possibly make. And it isn't practical to think in terms of paying cash for this kind of purchase.

George tells a story about a couple in his hometown who had the goal of buying a house for cash. Each time they got near the amount needed, inflation and rising costs had increased the price of houses. They rented for forty years, never quite making it, and then, in old age, moved into a convalescent home together, still renting.

Others have saved enough for a down payment, moved into a modest home in a good location, improved the house and land and sold for a profit, using that profit to move up to a better home, live in it, fix it up and sell it for a greater profit. Eventually, in this way, a couple can have their dream house.

Common Sense

> *I have to balance the books and make the money stretch. My husband is constantly overspending or investing unwisely. He'll say "let some bills go." He bor-*

rows money at 8% to 10% and leaves money in savings where it earns 5½%. What am I to do?

One woman turned the books over to her husband so he could see what was involved. He stewed and fretted over them until he had a stroke. When he recovered, he sued her for divorce. For her, that wasn't the right way to go.

See if you can get him to go with you to a reputable advisor in finance. He might be willing to listen to someone else who will point out to him that high-interest loans should be paid off with his "savings" which are bearing lower interest.

You might suggest also that he let you handle the money. You could budget it together, but you would be responsible for the actual disbursement of it.

Start educating him with stories of people who have made wise or foolish investments. Do it casually, lightly, offhand, so that he doesn't feel you are pointing at him. Some of this "teaching" may begin to sink in.

The Never Fail Investment

There *is* one, you know, and it brings great returns. Millions of people attest to its success and it's all wrapped around this comment:

> *It is hard for my husband to learn that God is the sole source of supply, not him, and God should be in charge.*

Not only is God the source, but God owns everything His children have or hope to have. He can turn off the spigot as quickly as He can turn it on. And one of the surest ways to make certain you always have enough is to invest your money in His work. In fact, He has exhorted:

"Bring all the tithes into the storehouse . . . and test me now herewith, saith the Lord of hosts, if I will not open for you the windows of heaven, and pour out for you a blessing, that there shall not be room enough to receive it."

That means giving at least ten percent of your money to church, to the poor, to missionary organizations, or to those who are working to populate the Kingdom of God by making people aware of the gospel of Jesus Christ. When you start doing this—taking it off the top—God gives back to overflowing. It's amazing, but it works! We have found it to be true in our own lives.

Insured For Life

My husband doesn't believe in life insurance. How do you feel about this?

Willy Worrier says he doesn't have funds with which to buy it. Carefree Al cites the Bible as his excuse, pointing out that Jesus said: "Don't worry at all then about tomorrow. Tomorrow can take care of itself! One day's trouble is enough for one day." But the Bible warns the slothful servant of impending punishment and further says, "If any provide not for his own house (his dependents) he has denied the faith and is worse than an infidel."

Too many times, widows and children have had to go on welfare and have been embarrassed because Papa suddenly died and left them with nothing. Life insurance is essential.

And Then There's The Estate

How should we go about making a will? Do we need a lawyer? Is there a simpler way to cut costs?

Everyone who doesn't have a will drawn up to suit himself has one in effect made out by the State. The State's Will is a set of rules directing the passage of property where the person has failed to give directions (in California, these rules are called the law of intestate succession). These directions are often contrary to a person's desires.

Most people have much more in their estate than they realize. You should have a competent lawyer help you complete your estate planning. You can minimize costs by contacting your favorite charity that has a stewardship department. Most such departments utilize aids for the gathering of estate data, have personnel trained to assist you in organizing this data and can refer you to a trustworthy attorney who will work with you to best accomplish your desired goals, properly.

Different Ideas

> *My husband goes overboard on buying farm equipment when we don't have the money. When we can't meet payments he says, "Don't worry. Something will come up." I keep the books and he says, "Don't worry!"*

Have you made certain that you understand what equipment is essential to keep the farm operating? If not, have your husband explain it to you in detail. Perhaps he feels it is necessary. On the other hand, you could go bankrupt if you move too fast. It would be wise if you worked out a reasonable plan together for adding equipment only when you needed it and when you can afford it.

> *We just don't have the same priorities when it comes to spending money. One of us wants to buy luxuries before necessities and before paying bills.*

People teach their children to desire luxuries by giving them first the sky and then the space ship to explore it while they're still growing up. This type of buying, at any age, is a poor way to go. Set goals together, budget your money, and stick to the program.

Junk or Gold Mine?

> My husband loves to go to auctions and spend money on "junk." It upsets me to no end.

Are you sure he's spending THAT much, or are you just irritated at what he does because it seems foolish to you? Turn his interest into an advantage! Join him, if he refuses to give it up, and turn it into a profit making venture. One couple we know studies antiques thoroughly and when they do buy, it is with discrimination. They have acquired some very beautiful items which have become worth many times what they paid for them.

MANAGING THE PAYCHECK

Even King Tut probably had his advisors. But some people set up little kingdoms for themselves in their own homes and expect the family to accept all their decisions without question. Such people are misguided. Here's an example:

> My husband says "I make it, I'll spend it my way!" Is that right?

Of course not. He hasn't learned what the word "marriage" means. In California, the law states that fifty percent of all assets belong to the wife. Maybe that's true in your state, too. He needs to be apprised of that fact. You are earning your half by keeping his home and children and being his wife. But if he still hangs on to this attitude, you will be much happier if you don't let it get to you. If he doesn't allow you to handle any money, including that for the house, you may wish to start a small money-making venture in your spare time so you can have some to handle yourself.

Here's a man who learned that it was much easier the right way:

> *I was closefisted and insisted on knowing where each dollar was spent. This caused much friction.*

I guess so! No woman or man should be subjected to this type of shabby treatment. Trust is all important. So is showing honor.

Foolish Spending

> *My wife does not use money wisely.*

Before you criticize her further, go shopping with her sometime, for food. And spend time with her in a clothes store. Men have very little conception of what a woman is struggling with when it comes to running a household. If she does make foolish mistakes like buying two poor quality dresses to save money when she should buy one good quality garment, or buying something on sale, even though you don't need it, you may have to explain a few facts of life to her. If so, keep exasperation and irritation out of your voice. Take a considerate approach and she'll not only love you for it, but she'll try to do as you say.

You Can Learn

One little wife says:

> *I have no business sense. It's a problem between us.*

You might have more than you know. It could be no one has bothered to sit down and explain business carefully to you. If your husband isn't good at that, or gets too impatient while trying to teach you, make it an over-coffee subject the next time you are with financially successful friends or relatives. You can teach yourself a lot, too, by reading books on the subject at the library.

She's Making Money

The independent working wife poses other questions. Some couples feel that's the way to get ahead but very often, little is gained. She must now have a much larger and better wardrobe than before. If she has small children she must get a sitter and that is a big hunk out of the take-home pay. (Very often, children who are left to the care of someone else give cause to the parents to regret it bitterly the rest of their lives). Add to that transportation and lunches out, plus a more difficult time having a family life, and the picture isn't too rosy. If she wishes to make money, it would be nice if she could go out on a part-time job or do something where she can work out of her home.

Besides, many women become resentful when they realize they are expected to work all day at a job and then come home and have the sole responsibility of all the other chores as well as child care.

Separate Bank Accounts

> Should a wife's salary be pooled with her husband's, or should her's be used for extras?

It gives a woman a wonderful feeling to make decisions about the money she makes. You don't *have* to pool it (unless you prefer to) but share with each other your goals and dreams, each taking certain parts of the financial responsibility. Be sure you have both of your names on all accounts. If one of you should die, it simplifies matters considerably.

Some people help spin the web that soon surrounds them. Here is a woman who has done that:

> *My husband spends the money he makes and part of what I make. My salary goes for household expenses. I work at three jobs besides my work at home to keep going. I feel like a workhorse being used by him. He has expensive hobbies that keep him away most of the time.*

Whoa there! Quit horsing around and go the other direction before you become bitter, ruin your marriage, or kill yourself with work. At least you ought to drop one or two of your jobs! If you don't have enough for household expenses, he may have to give up one of his expensive hobbies and that might keep him home more. But when you face up to him, please be kind at the same time you are being firm.

> *My husband gets angry because I am working and put my money in a separate account. I do this, because when we had our joint account, I kept the books and he gave me static continually.*

Many a man has blown his righteous stack because his wife couldn't keep the bank account to suit him. And most men feel nervous when there is money going in and out of an account over which they can't keep control. That's a cultural hand-me-down, we feel. It solves lots of family problems if the wife is given a separate household account to handle as she sees fit. She shouldn't have to even SHOW it to him, and when she needs additional money for the account, he should give it to her without questioning her judgment or honesty. When women are given this responsibility they usually do a fantastic job of handling it. She also can have extra money occasionally to buy hubby a gift without having to ask him for it, go to lunch with a friend while she is shopping or buy an extra blouse should she need it, without having to beg from Papa, which is demeaning.

It also gives a woman a marvelous sense of independence and maturity to have a little savings account of her own, as well. With it she can save up for something special.

> *How should a wife respond if her husband refuses to let her have or control a checking or savings account?*

With love and understanding. The idea of a wife having any say regarding financial matters may be completely foreign to him. Share with him your thoughts in this area. Ask him to give you a trial run. If he sees you are doing a good job and it is to his advantage, he will think no more about it.

P.S. from George: The Bible says the love of money is the root of all evil. Seems to me that things such as peace of mind and a love-filled home are much more important than getting rich. Agreed? Then let's act accordingly.

6

The Smooth as Clockwork Home

I'VE HAD IT UP TO HERE (WITH THIS MESSY HOUSE)

Should men do more housework, dishes, cleaning, scrubbing floors? Should they share in all the housework, or do the yard, or both? Should the woman share in the husband's work?

If you've read *Forever My Love*, you'll know that we shocked the socks right off a lot of husbands by suggesting they romance their wives into being better housekeepers, give them at least a day off a week to get away from it all, alone, and divide the evening chores up between them.

One fellow said, "I've had it. My wife just can't get it together. Do you know that every night it takes her until 9:00 o'clock to get the kids in bed and then she rattles around in the kitchen until 10:00 o'clock doing dishes? I can't even enjoy my T.V. program or read my paper in peace!" When it was suggested that a fifteen hour day might be a little much for her, he agreed, "I know that! But the work has to be done, doesn't it?"

No wonder women get sick of it. Husband, if you had to work fifteen hours a day at the same job, everyday, seven days a week, how would YOU feel? You've got unions to go to bat for you, but a woman doesn't! On top of that, if you are the efficient type, you undoubtedly married the inefficient type who just can't seem to organize. If so, she doesn't need your condemnation. She needs your help! The best way to help her is to compliment and praise her right into becoming a beautiful housekeeper. People become what you keep telling them they are! Critical Curtis says, almost nightly, to his wife, "I guess you'll NEVER be a good housekeeper!" I guess she won't either. But Happy Harry says, "Wow, honey, you can do anything you set your mind to, you know that? You're terrific. Just look at the way this living room is all slicked up!" Pumping that sort of information into her cranium for awhile will do the trick. She'll want her whole house slicked up! How do I know it'll work? That's the way George "trained" me when we were first married.

He DOES Help!

> *When you have tried helping your wife with the washing, cleaning, vacuuming, etc., done your yard work and jobs around the house, how do you get her to get off her dead end? She just says, "I wish I weren't so tired. You are just so good to help me." She won't ever do her housework.*

The clue to her behavior is "I wish I weren't so tired." A healthy woman doesn't say that. Take a good, hard look at our chapter on health (Nine: *Tired! Tired! Tired!*), start reading the books we have recommended, have her get a complete physical, including a 5-hour, 7-specimen glucose tolerance test to see if she has hypoglycemia. When one is saddled with the burden of ill health there is no way she can psych herself up to normal operation. Meanwhile, keep helping and get her a housekeeper once a week if possible.

Some Men Are Skeptical

One husband wrote us:

> *Okay, I'll read your book and do all the things you prescribed—for the next three months—and come home and find the sink full of dirty dishes. What do I do then?*

First, start thinking positively, instead of negatively. If you expect the worst, you'll probably get it. If you are critical, she'll give you reason to be. Three months isn't long enough to change what has been going on for years. Think in terms of "trying" for a year, sincerely loving, complimenting, helping and you just might see the caterpillar become a lovely butterfly, anxious to please.

He Won't

But it isn't always the lady that prevents the house from looking nice. One distraught woman cried:

> *I hate to keep nagging my husband about things that need to be done around the house. How would you suggest I tactfully handle this without being a shrew? If I don't say anything it just doesn't get done.*

Don't say anything. Just hand him a short list each week with a note: "Darling, these are things that are waiting for your expert touch. I'd do them but I can't as well as you, and I've run out of time. I love you so much . . . Jean." Keep a duplicate list. When he does something, cross it off the list. What he doesn't do, hand him the next week with a different note thanking him for what he did do, and adding on new things. If he continues to leave things undone, do them yourself or hire someone to do them. Maybe if he gets a few bills he'll decide it's cheaper to do the work himself. If he does something really important, prepare a fun time as a celebration.

He Tried For Awhile

> We live in an old house and I want to keep it clean, but no one else cares and I can't keep ahead of them. My husband hates shoes under the bed, but I have no storage space. When we were first married, he helped too much and interfered with my way of doing things.

You complained about your husband helping too much? Looks as if you threw the baby out with the bathwater. Now, no one helps you. We suggest that you look at your house carefully and plan some storage space. Tell your husband that you're sorry you didn't accept his help when he wanted to do it and that now you're paying for it. Show him your storage space plan and ask him to build it for you, or let you have it done, so you can have things put away as they should be. Also ask him if he will take over teaching the children to do their share—picking up, making their beds, washing out their tubs, etc. If you let him take over that portion of it, he could save you a lot of frustration, assuming you'll stand aside and not interfere.

What's Really Important?

> How can you help a husband to mature and find that a "spotless" house and a well made-up woman is not everything in life, but that the effort and the love put out while trying to meet the above needs sometimes take precedence?

If he is a perfectionist, it will be his nature to expect too much of others as well as himself. Spotless houses are for people who haven't learned to live in a home. Strive to have a neat, clean house for him each night when he comes home. Have everything in its place, and dinner on the table with the cooking utensils already put away. Then forget it. Take a bath, put on sweet smelling perfume and your makeup, fix your hair and wear an attractive outfit. If he still complains, just smile, kiss him and say, "I've done the best I can, honey. Now, come on, I've cooked a delicious dinner for you." Keep him off the subject by talking of happy, interesting things.

Dividing The Pie

> *Should a wife help her husband change the oil in the car if he helps her with the dishes?*

Do you need help?

MANAGING TIME

Corporations have seminars on this subject! They hire experts to come in at big salaries to see where employees are wasting time and suggest ways they can change. They are able to get things running more efficiently at the office, because each person concentrates basically on one job.

But what happens in the poor little home, where one harried housewife with several children is expected to be not only the butcher, the baker and the wardrobe maker but almost everything else you can name? No WONDER it's difficult.

Couple that unbelievable expectation with the possibility that she's the "creative" type and thus is, by nature, disorganized and you've got, most often, a messy house.

But don't despair, husbands! Don't despair, fun-loving little wife! We may not be able to make a coach out of a pumpkin, but we can help you get on schedule and have your home lovely before the clock strikes twelve.

Efficiency Plus

For starters, let's look at a sample day for a wife named Julie. Julie is an inefficient type from the word go. She has a baby, a toddler, and two children in school. Her schedule may not suit you exactly, but you can use it as a basis, and adjust it to fit your needs.

IN ALL FAIRNESS, let it be said that Julie's husband, Tank, did his bit by spending several weeks working with Julie, helping her clean the place from rafters to basement and making sure there was cupboard space built for every item. He even helped her organize the spaces! It's pretty hard to get efficient with a house that's topsy-turvy. So, we start with the assumption that your husband will do the same with you. However, if he won't, don't give up. You can still do wonders by yourself.

Julie will be able to keep her house exactly as Tank wants it if she'll stick pretty close to schedule starting with setting her alarm clock 15 minutes earlier than usual.

7:00 -
8:00 a.m.

1. Wake up, Julie! Thank God for safety and blessings.
2. Make bed upon arising.
3. Dress quickly in something neat, do a fast job on your face, comb your hair. (Uh uh. Out of the bathrobe! Out with the curlers. It'll take you twice as long to get moving if you don't.)
4. Baby's hollering. Run and change him. Get toddler to potty. Dress him.
5. Prepare breakfast.
6. Give baby something to chew on and toys to play with.

7. Serve breakfast. Make lunches while they eat. Oh, oh. Toddler is acting up. Feed him later, too.
8. Kiss all good-bye with smile and "I love you."
9. Put load of clothes in washer.

8:00 -
9:00

1. Now, feed the baby and toddler. Put toddler to work playing with the pots and pans cupboard, or something quieter, while you eat your breakfast. Allow yourself 15 minutes, reading Scripture or other inspirational material. It'll give you a good start.
2. Make list of things you need to do during day. (10 minutes only.) Put pots and pans back.
3. Take children with you. Make other beds. (Older children should have made theirs.)
4. Give bathrooms a quick once over (toilet, sink, pickup.) Let toddler help. Bathe baby, and dress him.
5. Set your hair. Let children play with curlers.
6. Throw wash load in dryer or hang on clothes line. (Fold clothes the minute they come out of dryer and you'll save ironing. Replace with permanent press.)

9:00 -
10:00

1. Make phone calls while you do dishes (you do have a 15 foot cord on the phone, don't you?) Limit calls to 5 minutes apiece. Keep eye on children.
2. Straighten each room. Everything goes in its place. (Every member of the family should be taught that whenever he leaves a room he should take something with him that belongs elsewhere.)
3. Bundle up children and go for 15 minute walk. Explore leaves and birds. Watch time.

10:00 -
11:00
1. Vacuum main areas where needed. Let little one help.
2. Run over kitchen and other floors with damp mop.
3. Sing a song.

11:00 -
11:30
1. Do odds and ends. Finish up house.

11:30 -
12:30
1. Make picnic lunch. Eat under a bush, or over there in the flower garden, or on the floor in the garage. Put a flower in the children's hair.
2. Clean up mess from picnic lunch.

12:30 -
2:30
REWARD TIME! Have all sorts of interesting things available to occupy children's time until naps.
1. Work on a hobby—you were going to start bird-watching, remember? Practice your guitar.
2. Nap when children do (20 minutes only for you so you'll have time to do some more on your fun things).

2:30 -
4:30
1. This is an exciting time, hearing all about the day at school from the older kids, looking at their schoolwork.
2. While they're jabbering, prepare dinner so it's ready to pop in oven.
3. After snacks, get them busy on piano practicing and work.

4:30 -
6:00
1. Older ones set the table and watch little ones while you shower, comb hair, put on fresh outfit (something really pretty). Laugh out loud while you put on perfume and count your blessings.
2. Get dinner in the oven.

6:00 -
7:00
1. Greet Daddy with lots of love and warmth. Keep dinner chatty and fun. Oh, you're going to watch T.V. while you eat? Then have a turn-off rule after one hour.

    2. Time for getting-dishes-done game. Everybody helps, including Papa. Set time. See if you can beat the clock.

    3. Now a quick run through the house to pick up toys, etc.

    4. Garbage out (older boy or Papa).

NOW! RELAXATION TIME!

Both of you can get the children to bed. Don't forget Bible reading and prayer!

VARIATIONS: Once you get your routine going and your house in good order, you'll be able to slick it up quickly on some mornings so you can do your grocery shopping. Limit yourself time-wise and shop in quantity, so you needn't go so often.

    You might wish to exchange baby-sitting with a friend so you can have one day free to do anything you wish (after the house is straightened).

SATURDAYS: Everybody works. Yardwork, hard jobs in house, fix and mend inside and out.

SUNDAYS: Sunday School, church, youth groups. Family Day.

Double Efficiency

Okay, Tank, here's your end of the bargain so she'll want to keep trying:

A.M.
    1. Upon awakening, thank God for the day and your blessings.

    2. Get up when your wife does. Help her make bed.

    3. At breakfast, spoon food into baby's mouth or help others manage while she serves and makes lunches.

4. Kiss all good-bye with smile, hold your wife a few seconds longer than usual and say, "I love you."

P.M.

1. Stop along roadside, in garden or in grocery store, and get Julie a little flower.
2. Relax for 5 minutes before getting home and just think of the GOOD things about your wife. Determine that, no matter WHAT greets you, you will keep a sense of humor and show lots of love.
3. Upon entering house, if kids rush you, love them, and ask loudly, "Where's Mommy?" Go to her immediately, hold her closely and say, "Hi, Beautiful!" or "I've missed you today." Hand her flower.
4. Tell children you'll meet them in 10 minutes, change into some good looking play clothes and have a 15 minute romp with them.
5. Join Julie in kitchen. Wash up pots and pans for her while she's finishing up dinner.
6. Keep dinner fun. No criticizing. Compliment her on something she cooked.
7. Afterwards, organize everyone to help with dishes. Make a game of it.
8. After dishes, help her with any other leftover chores.
9. FUN AND RELAXATION TIME.
10. Bible time.
11. Help Julie get children to bed. Prayer time!
12. Talk and dream together. Maybe make love, or . . . .
13. Spend an hour on one of your special hobbies.

On Time To Everything

One man boomed out:

She is never on time!

The Hardisty family has that trouble. *None* of us have trouble being on time when we are going to something alone. But when the whole herd is thundering about, the clock often beats us. If one of us isn't at fault, the other one is. Some personalities have more difficulty with time than others, and those who don't feel very self-righteous and irritated at those who do. The offenders are often the creative or fun-loving type of people who don't fit into molds easily. Since being on time is as foreign to their makeup as writing a symphony is to others', it is doubtful if they'll ever conquer the problem totally. But in order to live in a highly structured society and make more friends than enemies, they need to learn to plan and keep one eye on the clock.

If you are married to a wife like this one, see if you can come home early to help her in the areas that bog her down, when you two are going somewhere. Send her off to do her makeup and dressing, giving her at least an hour, taking over for her with the children, or house, or whatever. Put a clock on her dressing table and, with a kiss, a twinkle and a smile, say, "Now watch it, honey. I'm coming up to help you on with your coat at exactly 7:00." But be prepared to be calm in case she doesn't quite make it.

I Hate Being Told

How do you handle husbands who nag all the time about being late?

Start learning to be on time. Although it might irritate you to plan your time more efficiently and prepare ahead, you actually will be a happier person if you do.

Women Must Use A Different Approach

Can a wife help a perpetually late husband change his habits so he can be on time? He always starts getting ready too late. If I tell him this, it causes irritation. It is probably the source of most of our arguments. Saying nothing doesn't work either.

Can a leopard change his spots? Since it is unlikely your husband will ever be different (unless *he* makes up his own mind to be), it would be better if you quit agonizing over it. When you are invited somewhere, tell your hosts sometime ahead that you will be unable to be there until 15 or 20 minutes later. Don't blame it on anyone. Just state the fact. Quit criticizing and reminding him. Smile instead of looking accusingly at him. You're just bringing an unnecessary stress into your life. Use the waiting time to accomplish something you've been wanting to do. The fellow to blame is the one who decided to divide hours into minutes and seconds, way back when.

The Potatoes Are Getting Cold

How can I get my husband to realize how important it is to be on time for meals?

You and I are soul mates. George is a DOER. He accomplishes a tremendous amount in a normal day. And it all began when he was a kid. When his mother called him for a meal he would always finish the job he was working on before he'd go eat. He said that he thought of the meal as his reward if he worked until he got the job done. He hasn't changed.

I have my choice. Get upset or get with it. I decided long ago it was easiest to keep meals in the warming oven until he comes. Or, I call him 10 to 15 minutes ahead of time, as the meal is cooking. You can do the same. And think of this bonus: You will always have the distinction of eating later than anyone else in the county!

Putting Things Off

> *My husband is a poor organizer and a procrastinator. What can I do?*

Procrastinators have to do so much more work in life than others! The job they have of carrying around the knowledge that there is something they must do which isn't done yet is a much more difficult load to lift than if they were to just get it done when it comes up. On top of it, they face the disapproval and exasperation of those around them. The best cure is to have someone around them who cheerfully gets things done on time. Often, after a few years and a little maturing they'll see the benefit of it and start doing the same themselves. When a wife starts "reminding" and pushing, however, hubby will often dig his heels in and refuse to move altogether.

WHAT GOALS HAVE YOU SET?

Why bother with goals? Why not just rock along and enjoy life? Well, there's more than one reason to have a little ambition!

- You feel that life has purpose and meaning, essential to contentment.
- You get out of self and become of help to others, either by direct or indirect action.
- You are a more interesting person and find others more interesting.
- It makes sharing life with another easier.

We suggest three types of goal setting: daily, weekly and long range.

The daily goals are obvious:
> Call Aunt Myrtle
> Vacuum
> Clean bathroom, etc.

The weekly goal list might be:
> Go to bank
> Buy Buster shoes
> Call pastor
> Get x-rays of my toe
> As you make out your DAILY plan, add one or two things from your WEEKLY list.

Long range goals might be:
> Buy a house
> Write a book
> Visit South America
> Get acquainted with my neighbors
> Get puppy and train him
> Raise canaries
> Study art
> Become a bird-watcher

Each day, if possible, spend an hour or two on one of your long range goals. Going to buy a house? Start gathering real estate information. Going to start that book? Begin to gather research materials for your book. See what we mean?

George taught me the value of list keeping. True, I lose my lists consistently and usually end up with four, but it still helps me a lot. Otherwise, time is always just out of reach.

It's Easy To Let It Go

Often, only one of a team desires to set goals. For instance:

My husband and I have never really sat down and set goals for our lives. What we are really striving for. I have asked him two times if we could do this. But he takes offense if I bring something to his attention. What would be a good way for us to set goals without his thinking I'm pressuring him?

Forget about sitting down. Just talk with him about dreams and get him to share his thinking when you are relaxing together. Then quietly go about getting the ball rolling toward realizing those dreams. As you work on them, he may join you without your saying a word. He may even think they are his ideas if they're really good. If he still doesn't catch the vision, aim for goals of your own.

I have much drive and ambition regarding future needs. My wife has none. It's discouraging.

Discouraging? Why? You're obviously the leader and she the follower. Don't expect her to be like you. As you set your goals and work toward them, sharing your excitement over them with her, showing her the progress you are making and letting her know that she is part of it even if she doesn't take part, she may catch the fever and join in. If she doesn't, don't let it bother you. Just enjoy your accomplishments and let her enjoy the fruits of your labor.

Others Go At It Too Hard

We are over-committed. We need time to relax without feeling guilty.

GOOD for you! You've found the source of your problem. The next step is to take a good look at all you are doing, decide which things you are going to axe, and then axe them. You can tell friends that you have decided the family simply has to have more time together. Don't make the mistake one couple did: In their enthusiasm they cut out everything outside their home, became an island unto themselves and then began to get on each other's nerves. You need to give to others, some of the time.

Ah, Yes! Priorities

> *Would you talk about priorities in the home for the husband in relation to the wife, children, the husband's calling [I'm in the ministry] and financial obligations. Also wife's priorities.*

God always should come first in our lives, but not necessarily the activities that we often *attribute* to God. The enemy loves to keep you so busy in God's work that you haven't time to obey God in important areas of your life. God has led you into a ministry to help others and has felt it so important that this is where you make your livelihood. He also commanded you to love your wife and to supply her emotional needs.

I know pastors who plan one day a week when NO ONE is to bother them. Monday is a good husband and wife day. Let your secretary take any emergency calls and keep in touch with her. Since much of your life is on the run to supply other people's needs, your romance will have to be on the run, too. But you can still please your sweetheart with endearing looks, compliments, and encouragement for her to develop as an individual so she isn't living in your shadow or in a mold the church has set for her.

Your children need you regardless of anything else. When we see a "preacher's kid" who is troubled, very often we see that Papa has either expected him to be perfect and has been too harsh with him, or hasn't spent purposeful time with him on a continuing basis. Always be available to your children whether they have a problem or just want to share something exciting in their lives with you.

Keep your appointments with them.

Regarding financial obligations: You're no different than

anyone else just because you fill a pulpit. See our chapter on Money! Money! Money!

OUTSIDE ACTIVITIES

It's great if some of your special activities can be together. George and I have enjoyed traveling around the country lecturing. But we don't quarrel about who's going to do what. We know where our strengths lie. We just pool them and have fun using them. This couple would benefit from that type of approach:

> *Both of us love to entertain. But he won't help me plan the parties, so I just refuse to do it. What can I do?*

It's like the man who was riding the donkey to market to pick up some hay on sale and they came to a bridge, which was creaky and old. The man told the donkey, "You go first." The donkey protested, "No, you go first." They argued all day until finally all the hay was sold. They both lost. Perhaps your husband doesn't feel he's got the creative smarts for planning a get-together. Women tend to be detail people and can think of all the fun little things that men don't generally consider. If you aren't one of those women, get some party books at the library and consider new ideas. After you've planned an evening you can assign your husband some jobs, like setting up the tables, or shopping for the food, if he is agreeable. That would be more in his line.

> *How much entertaining should a wife do if there are children?*

Only as much as you enjoy doing. Include the children in your plans. They can help you prepare favors or blow up balloons.

When our children were growing up, we usually invited

families. We would hire a neighborhood girl to keep all the youngsters busy in a room set up with games, decorations and their OWN food and desserts, so we adults were free to enjoy ourselves.

If children don't come, yours can dress up and be put to work politely passing out nuts, candy and other unspillable things. If they are older they can help with directing cars or coat hanging. When the conversation becomes adult, or dinner begins, they may take their share of the goodies (laid out by Mom ahead of time) and retire to their own activities. It is good for them to learn not to run in and out of the room or interrupt. If they are tiny, you will want to have someone there to look after them until bedtime, so you are free to graciously entertain your guests.

Keep in mind, however, that although you think your children are the most intelligent, adorable creatures on earth, other people usually don't. They have their own idols. Don't force yours on them for any length of time.

Down, Girl!

> *I have a B.S. degree. So does my husband. I want to continue my education but he doesn't want me to go beyond him.*

Your husband seems to have a hang-up on male superiority, which is unfortunate. If you go ahead, he might adjust very nicely. On the other hand, it may be best for you to learn at home. Your life can be full to overflowing without it showing on a piece of paper. When he matures further, make it formal.

One college professor told me, "I have a husband and wife in my chemistry class. She's a whiz at it, but her spouse couldn't get through it if she didn't do his work for him. In fact, it's the same in almost every class he's in. She has begged me to give her a lower grade than his so he won't be crushed."

The wife is practicing sacrificial love. But she is being

dishonest. Her husband may not be able to outdo her intellectually, but he may have abilities that far outshine hers in another field—perhaps working with his hands. She would serve him far better if she were to help him discover his aptitudes and encourage him to develop in those areas, while she continues her education.

Anyone For Mozart?

> *I love music. So do three of my children. My husband doesn't. It causes dissension.*

Maybe he feels left out. I've heard wives say about their husbands (in front of them), "Oh, he doesn't know anything about music," or "He can't carry a tune in a bucket!" If you have done that (and you shouldn't have), he will resist music, probably all his life. That shouldn't stop your enjoyment of it with the children, of course, but try to have your sessions when your husband isn't around.

At the same time, consider: Is there something HE enjoys doing over which you haven't made a lovely fuss? Maybe you need to start that process. If you GIVE of yourself, for his sake, who knows? He just might get interested in your music.

Let's Not Be Ridiculous

> *My husband won't let me have any outside activites. I feel smothered.*

Most men who drag their feet on this issue are afraid that their wives will neglect their homes; get too independent and grow away from them; or will make them feel inadequate. You may have to take the initiative and sign up for a Bible class or join a ceramics group during the daytime hours. But be sure your home is neat and clean and his meals are delicious. He will soon see there is nothing there to frighten him.

Who's Most Important?

> *Because of my involvement with youth in work and extracurricular activities I never have enough time at home. How does one say no to the needs of others when one's family's needs may be neglected?*

The hardest word for any enthusiastic person who has a compassion for others is NO. We live in a world of sickness, sorrow, hatred, and strife. The need is great. But if you aren't careful, you'll find someone else counseling *your* family while you're off counseling others. If you went to a psychologist or an attorney for help, you would have to go during their working hours. People take advantage of you because you let them. Budget a typical week. Put your family's needs FIRST. That's only right. Then set certain times when you can counsel by phone, and certain times in person and stick with it.

He Leaves Her Out

> *I feel my husband is selfish when he doesn't include me in his hunting and other activities. I would like to go, too.*

I don't blame you. I love it. Have you asked him to let you go? If he agrees, be a trooper. Don't complain about the cold, the inconveniences or that he has whiskers he hasn't shaved off. Show him you're as rough and tough as the best of them even though you remain feminine. If he refuses to let you show your stuff, then consider that he may need to get off by himself and away from smothering togetherness. Take advantage of the situation and go have a blast. Visit museums, go to the symphony, or do whatever you've been wanting to do that he doesn't care about. Or maybe you can find some women that have the same problem and all of you can go hunting *yourselves*. Now, that'll be the day!

I AM A GOLF WIDOW. HELP!

Become a golfer. If he still doesn't want you along with him, get a woman companion and, when *he* goes, go to another golf course, with *her*. OR—use the time he is gone to do something you enjoy. If he is gone too much, and the children are being neglected, it's time for a good talk and the working out of a reasonable schedule, so he will share himself with them and with you.

She Hates It

> *I love to coon hunt, but my wife has no interest in it.*
> *I want her to share with me and get off my back.*

Women aren't usually drawn to sports where animals are treated cruelly. Is there a hunting sport you could engage in that gives the animal a more sporting chance? If you aren't about to change in that area, you'll have to expect your wife to be squeamish. You should find some other sport in which she can cheerfully join you.

Another very effective technique to get wives interested in hunting and other rough sports is to go to things with her that *she* likes: the opera, church socials, etc. If she feels you care about her desires, she'll be more likely to care about yours.

Meanwhile, Back At The Ranch

> *Some men are sports nuts and need fulfillment in this*
> *area. How can they watch their favorite sports and yet*
> *not have it be a conflict in the marriage?*

Women object usually because they feel neglected. The answer is to go out of your way to make your wife feel special in your life. Cut down your watching and spend time with her. (After all, she could go nutty on some project and neglect you, too! You wouldn't like that.) Then, when the big games come along she won't be against your seeing them, especially if you pop some corn and invite her to sit beside you so you can hold her hand, and feel her near you. Then when your side makes a touchdown, give her a hug and a kiss! If you GO to the games, take her along as often as she will go.

P.S. from Margaret: I'd *die* if George didn't encourage me to do exciting things! At least I'd die *emotionally*. He's a yummy husband.

7

Who's Running
This Show Anyway?

GOD'S PLAN

The Babylonians were remarkable people. You've heard of their hanging gardens, one of the Seven Wonders of the World. You may have heard of the impregnability of their city, so they felt safe from all intruders. Most certainly you have heard of one of their most famous captives, the prophet Daniel.

Capturing Daniel didn't signal their downfall, but something they brought along with him did: golden utensils. When Belshazzar came to power, he made a great feast and used the golden vessels that his grandfather, Nebuchadnezzar, had taken straight from God's temple of worship in Jerusalem. He served wine in them! And to add insult to injury he and all his guests praised the gods of gold, silver, bronze, iron, wood and stone while they drank from the goblets! Their merry making was brought to a hushed halt mid-feast as some fingers came forth out of nowhere and wrote a message on the wall, MENE, MENE, TEKEL, UPHARSIN. Trying to control his jellied knees, Belshazzar roared for his astrologers, and other wise men, to interpret the writing. They failed. His good queen remembered Daniel, who then quickly ruined the king's appetite for good. Daniel read the mystery words which meant:

> God hath numbered thy kingdom and finished it.
> Thou art weighed in the balances and art found want-
> ing. Thy kingdom is divided and given to the Medes
> and Persians.

And that very night, the unconquerable city was conquered. The enemy had come into the city by way of their source of water: a river which ran under the wall.

Maybe there is handwriting on your wall that you aren't reading! Like the golden vessels, perhaps the Bible, straight from God's holy throne, has been misused or ignored by you. Maybe you have felt it more important to follow your own wisdom and desires than those set out by God. If so, you can expect problems in your marriage, with your children, and ultimately with God, Himself.

Ouch!

There seems to be no Scripture to support the idea that the man is to be like a hammer that bangs down on the woman's head so she can chisel some sense into their rough-diamond children. That speaks of harsh, totalitarian rule which contradicts the directives given to the man to cherish his wife, love her as himself and supply her emotional needs. It has value when the man is weak and has not known or practiced his position as head of the wife, but put a tool like that in the hands of a man who is already overbearing and selfish and you have the beginning of trouble with a capital T. Many pastors have shared with us that they have had great difficulty dealing with this type of marriage in counseling sessions.

God appointed man to be head of the wife and the family

> . . . not because men are superior, and
> . . . not because women aren't capable,

but simply to keep order, and for man to act as woman's protector.

He did not intend man to *think*, *act* and *breathe* for the woman.

God Makes It Clear

In God's Plan, you, husband, are to—

BE THE HEAD OF YOUR WIFE. Her desires will be toward you. (This is her emotional weakness we've been talking about.)

> "For the husband is the head of the wife, as Christ also is head of the church . . .''

GIVE YOUR WIFE HONOR. It will crush her if you don't.

> "You husbands likewise, live with your wives in an understanding way, as with a weaker vessel, since she is a woman; and grant her honor as a fellow-heir of the grace of life, so that your prayers may not be hindered."

LOVE YOUR WIFE AS YOUR OWN BODY.

> "So husbands ought also to love their own wives as their own bodies. He who loves his own wife loves himself; for no one ever hated his own flesh, but nourishes and cherishes it, just as Christ also does the church . . .''

LOVE YOUR WIFE AS CHRIST LOVES YOU, BECOMING A SERVANT TO HER, for anyone who wishes to be served must serve.

> "Husbands, love your wives, just as Christ also loved the church . . . taking the form of a bond-servant . . . and humbled Himself . . ."

BE WISE AND DO THIS JOB WELL

> "Who among you is wise and understanding? Let him show by his good behavior his deeds in the gentleness of wisdom. But if you have bitter jealousy and selfish ambition in your heart, do not be arrogant and so lie against the truth. This wisdom is not that which comes down from above, but is earthly, natural, demonic. For where jealousy and selfish ambition exist, there is disorder and every evil thing. But the wisdom from above is first pure, then peaceable, gentle, reasonable, full of mercy and good fruits, unwavering, without hypocrisy."

Wow! What a husband that would be! What woman wouldn't want to do her part with that kind of man around!

But That Isn't All

Since God has declared that woman is the weaker vessel, the stronger one, the husband, must take the initiative, for woman's weakness will cause her to gladly do what God has commanded her, which is:

BE SUBMISSIVE TO YOUR HUSBAND. He has been appointed your head.

> "Wives, be subject to your own husbands, as to the Lord. For the husband is the head of the wife, as Christ also is the head of the church . . . But as the church is subject to Christ, so also the wives ought to be to their husbands in everything."

BE SUBJECT TO YOUR HUSBAND, LOVE HIM, BE A WORKER AT HOME.

"... encourage the young women to love their husbands, to love their children, to be sensible, pure, workers at home, kind, being subject to their own husbands, that the word of God may not be dishonored."

USE YOUR TALENTS, REACH OUT TO OTHERS, MAKE DECISIONS, BE A SPIRITUAL GUIDE AND LIGHT TO YOUR HOUSEHOLD, HAVE FAITH, SPEAK WITH WISDOM, CLOTHE YOUR FAMILY WELL, DO GOOD FOR YOUR HUSBAND, NEVER BAD.

"An excellent wife, who can find?
For her worth is far above jewels.
The heart of her husband trusts in her,
And he will have no lack of gain.
She does him good and not evil
All the days of her life.
She looks for wool and flax,
And works with her hands in delight.
She is like merchant ships;
She brings her food from afar.
She rises also while it is still night,
And gives food to her household,
And portions to her maidens.
She considers a field and buys it;
From her earnings she plants a vineyard.
She girds herself with strength,
And makes her arms strong.
She senses that her gain is good;
Her lamp does not go out at night.
She stretches out her hands to the distaff,

And her hands grasp the spindle.
She extends her hand to the poor;
And she stretches out her hands to the needy.
She is not afraid of the snow for her household,
For all her household are clothed with scarlet.
She makes coverings for herself;
Her clothing is fine linen and purple.
Her husband is known in the gates,
When he sits among the elders of the land.
She makes linen garments and sells them,
And supplies belts to the tradesmen.
Strength and dignity are her clothing,
And she smiles at the future.
She opens her mouth in wisdom,
And the teaching of kindness is on her tongue.
She looks well to the ways of her household,
And does not eat the bread of idleness.
Her children rise up and bless her;
Her husband also, and he praises her, saying:
'Many daughters have done nobly,
But you excel them all.'
Charm is deceitful and beauty is vain,
But a woman who fears the Lord, she shall be praised.
Give her the product of her hands,
And let her works praise her in the gates.''

That's right out of the Bible from a God Who understands women!

LET'S GET THIS STRAIGHT

Where does submission apply, practically speaking?

We might better ask, where does headship apply, practically speaking? A man who tries to juggle two full-time occupations (ruling every aspect of the household and filling his position at which he earns their sustenance) is going to do an inadequate job of each. So he wisely turns over one hunk of the responsibility to the wife who is to keep the house.

If the wife can't handle something, she can call on her husband and he steps in to assist. If he and she disagree on a matter, after discussion and exploring it thoroughly together, he must, as head, break the tie. If his wife is doing something harmful to herself or his children, he may have to step in with his authority and stop it.

The man's responsibility is big, for if he is to treat his wife as Jesus Christ treats the church, if he loves her as he loves his own flesh, cherishing and honoring her, when he makes a decision it will be for HER good, not his.

NOTE: We didn't say he is to always give her what she *wants*!

You can see now why many families aren't making it. Wisdom must be directed and given from ON HIGH, but too many men and women are following earthly teachings, and are ignoring God's plan.

Employer—Employee?

Let's take some real live examples where husbands and wives are wrestling with this problem:

> *Who's boss? I have a dominating wife and I believe as*
> *a result of this, I feel insecure.*

One woman we know is married to a man who had no father figure in his home to emulate. He isn't a leader. But she is a multi-gifted, talented woman who reminds one of a thoroughbred horse raring to go, and go she does! She's made her husband one of the wealthiest men in town, too. At the same time, he has gotten in and made his own successes; not as brilliant as hers, or as showy, but he's able to hold his head high. When she runs herself ragged, he steps in quietly and with concern. When she is asked to do something additional, she'll say, "My husband won't let me. He says I've taken on too much." Since he showers her with affection and love all the time, she stops when he says stop.

Enjoy your wife's gifts. You don't have to let her run YOU. If she tries, kiss her, tell her you love her and go on about your business as you see fit.

But when a man gets the idea he has to be a dictator, a bully or "boss" he's misunderstood the whole ball of wax.

Humiliation Hurts

> *Conflict between lack of submission by wife and humiliation of husband. I will give an idea and my wife will not submit. Must I humble myself to her idea?*

How about throwing an idea out and then asking your wife to talk it over with you? Allow her to explore all sides and angles of the idea, keeping an open mind. If she shoots holes in it, and you can see them, then why not show your maturity by saying, "Thanks, honey. I'm sure glad I talked it over with you. I can see how it wasn't all that good." However, after hearing all sides, if you still think you are right, you can say, "Sweetheart, your reasoning is good, but I still think I'm right. I'm going ahead with it and if I make a mistake, then I'll try to make better decisions next time."

Submission is certainly NOT insisting that your wife agree with everything you say! If she did that, she'd be terribly dull and not much of a helpmeet.

How Droll

> *Wife obey? What do you mean by obedience? Frankly, it sounds rather unadult.*

Unadult it may sound to you, but God says it. Therefore, if a woman wants God's blessings, she must heed. Actually, if a husband does his part as he should, there will be little problem. Women love a strong, leader-type man around, if he is just as adoring and demonstrative in his love as he is strong. It may surprise you, but many women are crying because their husbands WON'T take leadership in the home. Like this one:

How do I lead my husband to be head of the house?

You may not be able to "lead" him to be a leader. But you can help him improve by laying the responsibility in his lap. One pretty little wife, who is a strong personality, married a man who would just as soon sit and ruminate on the merits of sleeping or not sleeping. She started in as soon as they were married saying, "You'll have to ask my husband. He's head of the house," or "Make an executive decision, honey." You'll often hear her saying things like, "My husband is brilliant. He can do anything he sets his mind to." Their three children know Daddy is the final word.

She has kept up this barrage of positive comments and now, after ten years of marriage, he is a district manager for his company! He still isn't a man's man in the home, but when he feels it's necessary, he speaks his mind and expects his wife to listen. She goes merrily on her way, encouraging him, and where he refuses to lead, she fills the gap.

He Wants To Show Her Off

I know I should be submissive but my husband wants me to wear revealing clothes that are not my style. I am conservative in dress. He is not. What should I do?

Your first responsibilty, always, is to God. But in case you are simply digging in with your heels and stubbornly setting your jaw, let's learn to be clever. Wear revealing clothes when you and your husband are alone! When you are going out with him, wear garments which will show off your figure but which will keep you covered. When you are going out alone, you can be just as conservative as you desire. If that sounds like you'll have to have a larger wardrobe than some, perhaps that's true, but he asked for it, didn't he?

Just Do It

> My wife won't let me go fishing sometimes. We talk and talk about it, but she still won't let me go. What should I do?

What? Is your wife bigger than you? If you wish to go fishing, GO! If she punishes you by not speaking, or crying, or generally acting immature, that's her problem, not yours. HOWEVER, before you rush out the door, think this through. How much time are you spending doing fun things with her that SHE enjoys? When you go fishing, does that mean you neglect your duties at home? Do you go *every* weekend? Have you invited her to go along with you? Perhaps you need to make changes. But remember, your wife isn't the head of you! You're the head of her. After you have fulfilled your obligations at home, move out and become a man!

P.S. from George: Men who get hung-up on submission seldom are good at headship. Put your wife's needs first and she'll submit.

8

There's Another Side to the Coin

A MAN HAS NEEDS, TOO

Believe it or not, men DO have feelings other than the urge to take their wives to bed.

A friend studied her cup of tea, looked thoughtful and asked:

> *What causes us women to put our children's needs before our husbands'? We know we should do things for our husbands that we don't.*

It's true, I thought. For one thing, there is so much to DO that when husband arrives on the scene, there just isn't TIME! And somehow we feel he should be adult enough to REALIZE.

Furthermore, God has built into us an intense desire to protect and help our offspring. We LOVE them despite all the things they do to drive us batty. But wives and husbands allow themselves to QUIT loving each other when the mate doesn't shape up.

It's good to look a few facts straight in the eyes.

1. Your children will never love you as much as you love them.

2. They will soon be gone and you and your husband need to be friends, because you're going to be spending a lot of time together without distractions. Be prepared by putting him first now.

3. As you hold Daddy up as something special, your children will admire you for it. They will look up to him, and when you two are older, they will want you both around.

4. It's *fun* making a husband happy and supplying his needs.

Taking courage, a beleagured husband spoke up:

How do you tell a wife that she is super-critical of you and very demanding of her own way?

Some people are critical by nature. They are often as hard on themselves as they are on others, but any way you cut the cake, they aren't much fun to live with. You can do a few things to improve your situation, however:

● Swallow your pride and make a list of all the things *you* do that bother her. Sit down with her and tell her you are planning to change in as many areas as you can. Ask her to be patient, because you can't change overnight.

● Tell her kindly that when she criticizes you, it just makes you feel negative. Ask her to please look for the good things you do and praise you instead, while you are working to improve.

● Romance her with compliments, gifts, sweet, thoughtful gestures and words, telling her how beautiful she is when she smiles. She just might change.

Much as a woman craves the company of her husband, especially if her life is mainly a whirl of babies, thumb-sucking, dirty clothes, peanut butter and honey sandwiches and trying to keep up with the keeping up, she must be prepared to give a little more if she's married to a man like this:

> *What if you want to spend more time alone—maybe learning the piano, or just resting from the wife's chatter?*

You can explain to your sweetheart that you love her dearly and enjoy being with her, but sometimes you need to be alone to get your thoughts together, to think beautiful things about her, or work on a hobby.

Just as you are arranging for her to get a few hours off each week to pursue her talents, so she can tell the children, "this is Daddy's hour. No one is to bother him." Even better, perhaps the whole family can be taught the therapy of being alone to think or do for a special time, and when you all come together again, you might share a special blessing each of you got from your "quiet" time.

In every family there seems to be a generous helping of the "loudies" and the "quieties." As I look back, it seems that my brother John was his happiest while stealing through the forest like an Indian or fishing a mountain stream; my sister Natalie was a personage of unfathomable thought and a need for her own brand of solitude; and my sister Barbara usually hit the house and the piano like a happy hurricane. (I'm sure she deliberately passed her genes on somehow, some way to my daughter.) They all married opposites, as most of us do. Jackie wisely learned to become a crack shot on John's hunting trips, Norbert bought a little hideaway in the mountains so Natalie could get away from it all (although since then, he has joyfully invited everyone and his cow to visit, which they do), and Bob has learned to be an island of quiet while Barbara's enthusiasm jumps around him.

Couples have to adjust to each other and learn to give, but there's nothing wrong in carving out a little bit of what you need to help you be a better mate.

Something Besides Pancakes Is Needed

How do you get a wife to see that a pleasant send-off helps to put you in the mood to be happy when you come home?

It takes more muscles to frown than it does to smile. If more of us would smile when we get up instead of groaning about starting another day; if we could learn to recite ten blessings before we get out of bed; upon opening our eyes, if we could say, "Good morning, Lord. What wonderful things do you have planned for me today?"; if we could just whisper "I love you" or some similar sweet nothing to our mates as we part from them in the morning, all sorts of colors would burst in on blue Monday.

Since she isn't doing it, maybe you can begin. Try it for a few months, and if she doesn't catch the spirit by then, tell her in a tender moment sometime that you are concerned about her health. When she asks you why, you can say, "You're so pretty when you smile. And you seldom smile in the mornings. I want you to be happy all the time. I've been reading about that. Maybe you aren't getting proper rest. Whatever it is, I'll do everything I can to help."

Be prepared! She may meet that indignantly with a barrage of things you should be doing in the mornings so she CAN smile more. If so, do them!

Him, too?

My wife doesn't seem to need romance as much as I do and this makes me feel awkward. How can we both be satisfied?

If you're thinking of romance as sexual, then you aren't

supplying her with the kind of romance *she* needs so she'll respond to you, as you wish. But if you are the one who likes the flowers, dinners, sweet words, etc., why should you feel awkward? You are a sensitive person who has a real appreciation for beauty, and you should be satisfied. Nothing need change. Plan romance as any man should for his wife. If you enjoy it the most, you are one up on her and your next door neighbor.

A Bit Much

Look at this one:

> *Is it possible to get too much loving and patting and feeling from your husband?*

This lady signed her note, "Saturated." His need for expressing his love and receiving love by physical touch may be greater than hers. Or he may think that's the way to turn her on sexually. Seldom does pinching or patting a woman's posterior, or feeling her intimate parts when she isn't already aroused sexually, do anything but turn her off. Men have to be taught this. After all, women are nice things to pinch, pat and feel! A wife should frankly but kindly tell her husband what she does and does not like. Perhaps she could be more demonstrative with her hugs and kisses if he would be cooperative and knock off the repulsives.

Old Henry

Troubled husbands come in all shapes and sizes. Henry wasn't sure of his shape or his size. His wife wrote:

> *He's too self-conscious.*

Henry had to learn some mental gymnastics! It took some

doing but he finally came to the place where he could ACT reasonably normal in a given situation. He still has to fight "Old" Henry to give "New" Henry a chance. Like this:

Old Henry's thoughts upon entering a room full of people:

> *"Hmmm. They're all looking at me. I wonder if my pants are too baggy. Maybe my left eye looks funny. It FEELS funny. It must, or that fat lady wouldn't be squinting in my direction."*

New Henry controls it:

> *"Woops! I'm thinking wrong. She's probably squinting because she forgot her glasses and she's worried that I'm looking at her and thinking 'fat.' It doesn't matter about my baggy pants either. That fellow over there looks like he slept in his. Nobody's talking to him. I'll go over and introduce myself. He may need a friend."*

So many of our troubles begin in the mind, marching around like a victorious army, and if you aren't careful, they will conquer you without a shot fired. Some people say self-consciousness is just another form of pride, with self on the throne of the life.

He Can Do It Himself

Some men don't need to learn mental gymnastics. They already know it all. Flora asked us:

> *What can I do to help Darryl when it seems he doesn't want my help but really needs it?*

Women need to be needed, don't they? But men need to believe they are strong and can do it alone! Be content to help where he'll accept it, and to continue to help him without making it obvious when he won't.

George is a man who knows where he's going in life, why he's going there and what time he'll arrive. I learned a good portion of self-confidence from him. Needless to say, he is a totally self-sufficient male, a most frustrating thing to a woman who has an instinct to mother. He even takes his own temperature when he's ill! I've learned that if I want him to consider my ideas and go along with them, I must drop them into his thinking before his mind is made up about what he intends to do. If I make it before the deadline, he is compliant and reasonable. If I miss, I might as well hang up my hat and forget it.

Self-sufficient he is, but invincible he is not. Sometimes he should have listened. Other times he gets along amazingly well without my advice.

To give you an example, two years ago, we bought some bare root trees: a fig and an almond. Not realizing the time (which is usual for me) I failed to put my bid in for where I wanted them to be planted. In dismay I stood looking at them later. The fig had been planted directly under the branches of one of our old apricot trees and the almond directly under the branches of another old apricot tree. His reasoning was that the apricot trees would die, we'd cut them down and the new trees would already be in place. I just KNEW they would grow up warped and squatty. But, as he predicted, both apricots popped off from old age and the little trees are cheerily holding their own.

But More Than Anything

More than his personal wants, even, man's need is to realize how easy it is to do something about the patchy places in his marriage.

From Southern California came this comment: "When you

counseled with me, I was only there out of politeness. I told you I knew my wife would change if I did those things, but I didn't want to bother. Then I began to feel badly about it so I've decided to give it a try. Already there's a difference. I wish I had started sooner.''

Rory visited our church one morning so he could meet us. He ran up with arms outstretched and a big grin on his face. ''You will be forever my love for showing me how to make my marriage super. If I had known my wife would react like she has, I would have started LONG ago. At last things are going MY way because I made things go HER way.'' What is true for him can be true for you, as well.

THAT JOB OF HIS

It's enough to make a man's head whirl! His wife sends him flying out the door every morning with the battle cry, ''Go and get ours, honey!'' And then she complains if he spends much time doing it! Right or not, though, a certain amount of juggling must be done, because if he isn't making it at home he won't be doing as well as he could at work. If there's conflict in the nest, there are a lot of temptations away from the nest that will present themselves when he gets up from his desk to stretch. That can lead to a very messed up life. So, it behooves both men and women to keep the home fires contained so they warm and don't burn.

Here's a man that needs to take a second look:

My husband holds down two jobs. He has no time for home.

What's responsible? Are you terribly in debt? If so, look at our chapter—MONEY, MONEY, MONEY. Are you trying to get ahead so you will have more material things? Re-evaluate your lives and your priorities. We have known families that have broken up because the husband holds down two jobs. It's better to do without some things, or wait for them, than to take that chance.

Not that we're encouraging you to present him with an unpleasant threat. If it's possible that the work will be temporary, be willing to wait and make each moment you can have together memorable and pleasant.

Another alternative is for you to offer to work part-time during the day so he can be relieved of one job.

The Independent Businessman

> *When a person is involved in a new business and his time is very limited for the wife and family (this is causing conflict), how can he find a balance?*

We know what you're talking about. Attorneys could work twenty-four hours a day, seven days a week and still not get it all done! Fortunately, George determined early in marriage that weekends and part of each evening were to be reserved for his family and he hasn't had to violate that very often.

Anyone who's his own boss has to work longer hours than a person on salary, but if you don't pull on the reins now, you'll find, after the business is well on the way, you never will! There will never be *less* demands on your time!

There's nothing wrong with a long day and late dinners, but be home in time to wrestle with your children and to have a talking or sharing time with your wife before bedtime. If you must work some of the weekends, bring the work home if possible and set aside a few hours for it on Saturday, but keep weekends basically for your loved ones and getting home chores done.

It's A Long Day

> *From when I leave for work in the morning until I get*

> *home in the evening takes about twelve hours each day. When I get home, both my wife and I are very tired. If I don't get some kind of rest before I go to bed, I am unable to work well the next day. So there is no time to help around the house. How can we work out this problem? I can't change the work hours.*

We're almost on the same schedule as you, except we are able to cut it down to eleven hours some days! It hasn't bothered us at all. I welcome the extra time to work on my things, and George is able to accommodate clients who find it very difficult to get off work during regular work hours.

Consider two things and please don't throw something at us:

1. Is there a possibility that you've been looking around at others who have shorter days and are feeling sorry for yourselves? Negative thoughts can make the body TIRED!
2. Have you checked your health lately?

If you still can't get on top of it, try budgeting your time just like you budget money. Consider public transportation, or, second-best, a car pool. Once you get used to the few inconveniences, you can spend that traveling time dozing, reading, having devotions or stimulating your mind with conversation. That might allow you to have enough energy to help your wife and children with dishes after the meal, or other chores, so you both can have some relaxation time.

When I was a school teacher, I learned a valuable lesson from my roommate. Everyday, when we had finished a day of wrestling with the minds of those little balls of energy, Cathy would lie on her back, spread some newspapers over herself and doze off. I was amazed!

But after I had the exhausting job of caring for two little ones of my own, I learned the value of a twenty-minute doze. It does wonders!

Set aside a half hour each evening for play time with the children—a family game, wrestling or sharing a picture book.

Seriously consider what really is important in your life. Maybe you need to move closer to your place of business so you can cut commuting time. Perhaps you ought to be looking for different employment so you won't be a slave to the job.

God Gets Blamed For Everything

> *God gave me a job that puts me on call twenty-four hours every other week. Sometimes it's necessary to work 80 or more hours in a week. I travel on business out of town and my wife can't come most of the time. My wife and I have tried repeatedly to put our family and spiritual life on a schedule only to have it devastated by an assignment. How can we better cope?*

Forget the schedule. Have a number of things planned ahead for your spiritual times. Enjoy your devotions and family times on a spontaneous and fun basis. Perhaps you could have a grab bag set up so that when you think you are going to make it through an evening without a call, you can have one of the children draw a suggested activity out of the bag. Since the items needed to go along with this suggestion are ready to go and waiting on a shelf somewhere, you're all set! If you are called away before you get started, then tell the family "We'll do this first thing when I get back, and on top of it, I'll bring a little surprise to go along with it!" The surprise can be something to munch on, a new little Bible storybook, or a Scripture game. If you have no way of buying it while you are gone, have your wife shop for it and give it to you to present to them when you come back.

While you're gone, your wife can carry on with devotional times every day with the children. She can keep the family in order. Let her help you carry some of the burden.

We're often intrigued with what traveling evangelists and the like have to do to keep their families in some semblance of spiritual growth and so they won't resent what takes Daddy away. Some call their families nightly from wherever they are. The cost is more than worth it. Everyone talks to father, shares some treasure and can make a complaint and get his advice or sympathy. It also keeps *him* current so that when he charges in the front door, he doesn't feel like a stranger or upset everyone's routine. If you can't call every night, make it every other night.

> *My husband spends six days a week at work and I am left with the excessive burden of responsibility. I'm at my wit's end. What should we do?*

The llama is a cute little fellow who refuses to move if he's expected to carry too many things to market. Off comes a basket. Nope, he still won't budge. Take the blanket away! Ah, that's better. He turns those soft eyes on his owner with a silent thank you and heads down the mountain. In your case, you can't use exactly the same tactics. You may end up with trouble for which you didn't bargain. But you can change some conditions yourself.

Seldom is it necessary in these days of unions to spend six days at work unless a person really wants to do it. The indispensable employee hardly exists anymore.

There is a possibility that overwork is your husband's way of avoiding being at the house. Take a good look around. Is your home a cheerful, happy place, or does he hear you sighing and complaining more than laughing and encouraging? Do you have nice little surprises waiting for him once or twice a week? Use your imagination. Wrap up a tiny little box in pretty paper. Inside put a candy kiss and a note—"I think you're the greatest!" Make his favorite meal and have it later without the children, under the charm of candlelight. Arrange to let the kids get away for a few hours on Saturday, if he'll stay home, so you can make love after a special lunch together.

If he's working to pay bills, budget yourself more closely and save the extra money to present to him in a special envelope each month.

After you've made home a fun place to come to, then decide just what you both want out of life (See Chapter Six—What Goals Have You Set?) If his goals are different than yours, then you must operate more independently. But maybe he will see that enjoying his loved ones while he still has them is more important than being the most conscientious man at work, and that the overtime pay isn't worth it.

Pack Up, Ma!

> *We've moved eleven times in twenty-two years be-*
> *cause of my husband's job and I'm sick of it. What*
> *can I do?*

Some friends of ours in a similar situation felt compelled to stay with the company. They had to think of seniority, retirement benefits, security, wages and all that goes with having a job with a good employer. After they were moved by the company the last time, the husband finally decided he had had it. He looked around, found a younger, more flexible company which was glad to have a man of his experience and expertise, quit the job he'd had for twenty years and stepped into a high managerial position with the new group. His wife was delighted, and the family life is in a stable position for the first time in years, which ironed out a lot of problems.

Share this with your husband. If he still refuses to consider something else, change your thinking before it ruins you and your marriage. Be glad you have a husband who provides for you.

One wife we know, whose husband is in the service and has to move frequently, smiled when someone commented about how sad it was she had to move after just getting settled nicely. She said, "I love it! I get to meet so many people, and the Lord always has something very special for me to do everywhere we go.'' That's keeping a positive attitude.

No man should work at something that makes him miserable if there are other alternatives. Life is too short. But here's a different slant. Another wife protests:

> *I married a professional football player and a lot of what he does in his job doesn't agree with my ideals. (Attitudes, habits which he picks up from other players.)*

You'll have to be extra watchful that your husband has a strong spiritual influence at home. He needs to be much in God's Word to keep steady morally.

Be sure to have him read articles and books telling about different Christian athletes. Campus Crusade for Christ International often has articles of this sort in their magazines *Worldwide Challenge* and *Athletes In Action*. Write to them for information about their international organization of Christian athletes. [2] Be very beautiful for him at home. Change your hairdo frequently. Make sure your wardrobe accentuates the best in you. Help him resist temptations by being the biggest temptation he knows.

Some women need a soft boot in the right place to get them moving:

> *How can I get my wife to realize how important it is that she attend social functions with me?*

What's bothering her? Maybe she doesn't feel that her clothes are up to par with the other women. Give her enough money, if that's the case, to update her wardrobe with a few

---

2. Campus Crusade for Chirst, Inc., Arrowhead Springs, San Bernardino, California 92414.

really nice pieces. Maybe she feels she can't compete hair and make-up wise. Have her go to a hair stylist and make-up artist. Or she can buy a top quality hairpiece for a special look. Does everyone get potted at these affairs? Perhaps she doesn't like it, and we don't blame her, but . . . .

HERE'S a word to *her*: If you are resisting just because it's too much effort, may we remind you that there are lots of women out there in the big wide world who would love to take your man away from you. Guard your property! Go with him! Besides, maybe there will be some people there who need you to listen to their troubles. It can become a real challenge.

P.S. from Margaret: Our pastor, Harold Carlson, often says, "I'm for you!" Well, we're for you, husband. We're for you, wife. We're for your getting it all together so your relationship is a JOY, not just a ho-hum existence.

9

Body Beautiful

I SWALLOWED A BALLOON

It is apparent to me that I'm not the only lady who has a problem with weight. I honestly want to lose, and my husband wants me to. Why can't I? Or why won't I? I feel like giving up. Help us women.

She was right. It was apparent. Many women waddled into our meeting and others looked like they had reached for the second helping too many times. The men were the same, but it wasn't such a bother to them. Women are continually fighting the bulge trying to keep attractive so their husbands will keep on loving them and to some it becomes a nightmare. Besides that, too much weight can cause miserable health problems.

Since overweight is a result of different influences for different people, what works for one may not work for another but give these suggestions a try and see what happens:

1. Look into the new diet drinks that are ALL NATURAL and brimming with vitamins and minerals.
2. Start reading up on nutrition (see our Bibliography). By

building health through proper nutrition, weight will be lost more slowly than if you were on a crash diet, but what you lose will usually stay lost.

3. Get a sympathetic doctor to treat you.
4. Get your husband to help. He can hold out rewards for you on short-term and long-term bases: Five dollars for every pound you lose (oh, come on now, husband, it isn't THAT much when you consider the rewards! Divvy up!); A new dress for every ten pounds; a full wardrobe when you lose the full amount; or something else you've been hankering for all your life.
5. Get your husband to help again. Ask him to forego desserts that have anything fattening in them so you won't be tempted. He'll be a lot better off with fresh fruit anyway and if he feels desperate, he can always get a snack downtown during the day.
6. Start thinking happy thoughts and singing throughout the day and evening. Start working on some interesting hobbies so you can get away from the humdrum of your daily routine.
7. Avoid meetings and social invitations where you will be tempted to eat. Explain it to your friends, and ask them to invite you back next year when you are a new you.
8. Get a friendly weight-losing group started at your church or home. You can encourage each other by setting goals together.
9. Don't rule out counseling. Maybe you've got a deep-seated psychological problem.

Saranita, a friend who helps me secretarially, told me that there was a time when she wanted to be slim and trim but eventually she had to face up to the fact that she just wasn't

BUILT that way. She pointed out to herself that in some countries, the buxom lass is more preferable to the boney one. She came to the conclusion that, for her build, she was NOT overweight. What a relief it is to get to where you not only accept but LIKE yourself, just the way you are.

Keep in mind: Some men prefer a big armful! If yours does, stop fussing.

TIRED—TIRED—TIRED

Typical of complaint after complaint is this one voiced by a disgusted husband:

My wife is too tired for sex, too tired for housework, too tired for anything! I think she's just lazy!

It is so difficult for a WELL person to understand or have patience with one who is ill. We tend to judge other's actions from personal experience. There are many physical ailments which can make a person tired but we would like you to consider the possibility of one in particular. Let's let some real-life situations speak to this: One young man who was a physical education teacher in a large high school told us,

I got to where I couldn't get my legs to move, it seems. I'd drag myself to school, try to do my work, but it was obvious that if I didn't stop, I would drop. So I got a leave of absence. After much testing and physical examinations, one doctor discovered I had hypoglycemia

> *(low blood sugar). I'm on a diet now and taking vita-*
> *min shots as he tries to rebuild my organs. It's been a*
> *year now and I feel better but I'm still far from normal.*

One couple, who sponsored a seminar we were conducting shared over a midnight snack:

> *Our daughter is fifteen. She seemed to change over-*
> *night from a sweet, happy child to an angry, depres-*
> *sive, disrespectful, disobedient nightmare. We were*
> *desperate. We took her to six doctors, all of whom re-*
> *fused to give her the glucose tolerance test to see if she*
> *had low blood sugar. Finally, in desperation, we read*
> *everything we could get our hands on, changed her*
> *diet and within a few months had our daughter back*
> *again. It worked like a miracle.*

Is Hope Gone?

> *Our sex life has diminished to nothing. We have just*
> *discovered that my wife has hypoglycemia (low blood*
> *sugar). Is there any hope in the future?*

The answer is yes. Read on.

Our doctor, one of the pioneers in this field, feels that eighty percent of the people walking the street suffer from this condition. Another doctor told me he believes a high percentage of mental patients in our institutions are there because of this malady. It results from stress and runs rampant largely because of our high carbohydrate, high stimulant diets. Although it is common, it is serious, for it affects several vital organs which, if the abuse continues, will weaken or give out, making the victim susceptible to attacks from other diseases. Happily enough, it can be cured and controlled by diet, proper vitamin and mineral intake, proper rest and cutting down on emotional, physical and chemical stresses.

When I was struggling with the logistics of the thing, a friend who had nearly died from it tried to explain it in a down-home language:

> *"You see, Margaret, if you eat a candy bar, the sugar in it causes your blood sugar to rise rapidly and high. The pancreas is designed to shoot out insulin into the bloodstream to balance things out but when TOO much concentrated carbohydrate is taken, it sort of panics and shoots out so much insulin that ALL the sweets are gobbled up, the blood sugar level drops way below normal and you are tired. So you take a cup of coffee to give you a spurt of energy. The same thing happens. If this is going on, day in and day out for years, your poor organs decide it isn't worth it all and begin to give up."*

Homey illustration and not very scientifically stated, but it gave me a hazy idea of what was going on inside and how important it was for me to resist some of the things I crave. Since then, I've learned to serve fresh fruits for dessert or make desserts with minimum sweetening.

While you're researching material concerning this subject*, let me pass on to you a few things I've been instructed to do to keep mine under control:

DIET: Sugar, caffeine and too many starches are poison. Natural sweets, as in fresh fruits won't hurt, if eaten in small amounts. Very small amounts of starch are okay. No liquor, coffee or tea (except herb teas).
Increase *protein*.
Increase foods containing lipids (fatty food substances). Excellent source: raw *fertile* eggs. Take 6 to 8 daily.

PHYSICAL: No strenuous exercises until well. Walks, relaxed swimming and other similar forms are good. Nap and get extra sleep at night.

CHEMICAL: Drink non-fluoridated water. Choose foods without preservatives in them. Avoid breathing aerosol products. No smoking.

EMOTIONAL: Avoid conflicts as much as possible and keep your cool during them. Keep calm in emergencies or times of grief if you can.

If you suspect either of you have hypoglycemia, search for a doctor who is knowledgeable on the subject and have him give you a five hour, seven specimen Glucose Tolerance Test.

Caution: One family took their son in for the test. The doctor's interpretation of the curve indicated that he didn't have low blood sugar. Not satisfied, they took the results to a doctor in another city who is an expert in the field. He and his partner studied it and both declared "without a doubt" he was a victim. So, even though the standard tests don't show it, according to your doctor's interpretaion, you need to consider the possibility that you may have it anyway. After all, it wouldn't hurt ANYONE to cut down on the four "S's": sweets, starches, stimulants and smoking.

* Detailed information regarding hypoglycemia may be gotten from Dr. Alan Nittler, P. O. Box 838, Soquel, CA 95073.

And Then There's The Weed

My husband refuses to quit smoking. I know it is harming him. The children want him to quit, too.

Our son gave a speech in his college class on smoking which stimulated a lot of discussion. His facts were those which have caused alarmed people to make their voices heard. As a result, airlines section off part of their planes for non-smokers, anti-smoking campaigns have run full tilt and "No Smoking" signs appear in many places.

The American Cancer Society is loaded with enough evidence against smoking to sentence it to capital punishment several times. We're convinced that smokers aren't at it simply because they enjoy it (many of them don't) but because they are hooked, despite the old familiar, "I can quit anytime I want. I quit last year for a whole week. No problem." If you are one of those who is honest about the situation, you can get help.

Where?

The American Cancer Society recommends several organizations who are set up to help you get rid of this deadly habit. Contact them for information.

One of the biggest incentives to your stopping, if you aren't concerned about your own health, is the health of your children and people around you. Regarding cigarettes, pipes or cigars, the American Lung Association puts out a leaflet which states that side stream smoke—the smoke from the burning end—has higher concentrations of noxious compounds than the mainstream smoke inhaled by the smoker.[3] They have many fascinating facts to back them up. It's just downright inconsiderate to force others to smoke when they don't want to.

Actually, you have my sympathy! I tried to quit *coffee* some years ago and although I seldom drank more than one cup a day, I had to admit that I was hooked on the lift it gave me to get going! About that time I began researching the crucifixion story which I was doing for radio. I read that the women of Jerusalem mercifully would take wine mixed with myrrh (a stupefying drink) to the crucifixion prisoners so it would lessen

3. *Second-Hand Smoke*, American Lung Association, 1740 Broadway, New York, New York 10019.

their pain. But Jesus refused everything offered Him. It hit me that if He could suffer the fullest for my sins, so that I might have life, then the least I could do was give up a cup of coffee for Him. That did it. I never needed a cup of coffee after that.

Becoming aware of hypoglycemia or the need to stop smoking is hardly an answer to all health problems! Not only are there a host of diseases and ailments, but there is the unbelievable influence the MIND has over the body. The MIND, if it thinks wrongly, can make the body operate wrongly. And, even though it seems we are playing ring-around-the-rosy, the truth is that the body can make the mind move in unhealthy channels.

Depressed

I can see him yet. We were speaking at a dinner meeting in New York when I looked down and there he was. He looked like death warmed over and I compared him mentally with a character I saw in a horror movie one time. Imagine my chagrin when he made his way up to the front for counseling. But the gnawing unpleasantness soon disappeared as the poor fellow shared his sorrow with me.

> I was forcibly retired from a job I loved. I am depressed and utterly defeated. I can't do anything anymore. I have no wife to help me. Can you?

So much illness begins in the mind. Anger, hatred, depression, fear and other emotions can destroy us. Depression is not unconquerable. If this is your problem, we suggest the same things we passed on to him. Start by going through the Bible and underlining all the promises God has made to His children, and then claim them for yourself, repeating some audibly every day. Force yourself to smile. When a negative thought comes in, say "Thank you, Lord, that You are working it all out."

Pour yourself into the lives of others, sealing your lips regarding your own troubles. Offer them encouragement.

Seek professional help, read books on the subject and get a complete physical checkup. Oftentimes a change in diet helps.

Relatives who live with depressed persons need to be very patient, kind and encouraging.

P.S. from George: Not everyone is going to get well. In that case, it seems, we might try to do everything we can to make sure OUR struggles don't make life MORE of a struggle for others. Keep smiling.

10

Children Can Be A Pain

A TROUBLEMAKER IN EVERY FAMILY

Surprisingly, on the sheets we passed out in our seminars and lectures on marriage difficulties many women listed "children" as one of the main causes of friction in their marriage. Only a few of the men agreed. The difference in opinion is understandable. A woman must deal with the children probably three times as much as the man. She can look back on the day's events, and dancing before her eyes, like spiders hanging from a chandelier, are things she would rather forget: Baby refused to eat one nutritious thing all day; five year-old threw sand in the neighbor five year-old's face; nine year-old didn't do one thing he was asked; thirteen year-old argued and sassed, and then when Dad came home, ran to him with her side of the story, and he bawled mother out for not understanding the poor little thing.

On top of it, it seems there is usually one child in every family who wants to swim upstream when everyone else is going down. He or she is the one who always has to learn things the hard way, because advice is seldom heeded and usually despised. They don't want to be put in a mold. They are the wild colts and parents have to learn to ride them without breaking their spirits.

To write about children and the problems they cause needs another whole book, but we will touch upon some of the areas where people seem to need help the most and give it a surface treatment.

Disrespect

Echoed by parents all over the nation are questions similar to this one:

> *How can I make our children obey better and stop mouthing back to me when I tell them to do simple little everyday chores?*

Earl Jabay in his book, *The Kingdom Of Self*, makes the observation, "It is absolutely crucial that the child does not win in its clashes with authority. The mother of John Wesley declared that the will of a child should be conquered by the time he is four years old."

The grim, cold authoritarian type of parent who administers the whip everytime his offspring squeaks the wrong way is obviously not the answer. He leans heavily on the saying, "Spare the rod, spoil the child." Many of the most viciously hateful delinquents come from that type of treatment. Neither is the permissive, do-anything-to-keep-peace parent going to make it. This type of parent is told in the Scriptures that he who doesn't discipline his child hates the little darling no matter how much ohing and ooing they do over him.

There seems to be a little of both type of parent in the best of us. We blunder on one side and then on the other. Consistent discipline is what we KNOW we should use, but unfortunately, our brand of dealing is affected by our health, our emotions, whether or not something GOOD happened to us that day, the time and the hour, and a host of other variables.

Furthermore, we get *angry*. A lawyer knows that if he loses his temper while trying a case in court, his opponent has won the battle. No wonder the child, who already is establishing his kingdom and daring anyone to cross the moat, is confused.

Don't despair, though. We've all been through it. The Hardisty's have had their share of royal battles and we haven't always come out winners. When we see how our children turn out, we'll write that first book on child rearing.

God has the answer, of course. It's a mixture of firm, loving training, holding out rewards, holding back privileges, spanking or not spanking. The catch is to remain loving when you feel like knocking heads together. Praise God and thank Him for what He's going to do in your children's lives everytime you are temped to be discouraged, angry or critical. That takes a CLOSE, CLOSE walk with the Lord—all day—all the time.

Tale Carriers

If you start to see undesirable qualities in children, are they reflections of yourself and the relationship between husband and wife?

Emphatically yes. And emphatically no. When we see a look on the face of one of our children during a conflict, and accidentally glance in the mirror, we will usually see the same look on our faces. In one word, ugly. If a Dad doesn't romance Momma and isn't kind and loving to her, chances are the son will treat Momma and his future wife the same way. If Momma defies her husband and verbally sets him straight from time to time, daughters may follow suit with Daddy and, after they're married, their husbands. Children learn much about loving and hating, industrious or lazy behavior and exhibiting inner strengths and qualities, by watching us.

On the other hand, every child has his own personality, and nature, just like adults do, which the Bible calls wicked: "The heart is deceitful above all things and desperately wicked; who can know it?" And every child will eventually be responsible directly to God, not for how his parents treated him, not for how society treated him, but for his own actions and intents of his heart. It will be up to him whether or not he surrenders his life to the ONE who created him and loves him and wants to give him eternal life, or to the enemy who so cleverly leads astray and into destruction. Since he stands alone on this threshold and his parents are powerless to determine whether or not he will enter heaven, it is essential for them to prepare that child spiritually, to make sure his heart and mind are saturated with the Word of God, to be certain he is surrounded by others of like mind, and to PRAY, PRAY, PRAY, BELIEVING that God will break through the opposing forces and rescue the little lost lamb.

There's More Than One Reason For Bad Behavior

> *How can we get our 8 year-old girl to obey better? The child is very active. Doesn't want to sit still. Doesn't want to be quiet when told. This happens at home, shopping, church, restaurant, anywhere, and it affects us both and irritates her teenage brother. We've tried every form of discipline we can think of. What have we missed?*

Dr. Clyde Narramore, noted Christian psychologist, is often heard to say, "All behavior is caused."[4] Your child could be neurologically impaired, and you may be expecting her to do something she simply can't do. We know of several families whose children are being treated medically for this. See a neurologist. Chiropractors are doing extremely effective work in this area too, without the use of medicine.

Sometimes diet is all-important. Does she eat or drink lots of

---

4. Dr. Clyde M. Narramore, Psychologist, Booklet #28—Children With Nervous and Emotional Problems, Narramore Christian Foundation, 1409 North Walnut Grove Ave., Rosemead, California 91770.

sweets? If so, you might consider taking her off of them.

This child needs much love and acceptance. Try to ignore as much of her behavior as possible, so she won't suffer a preponderance of criticism. Concentrate only on the important infractions.

A Word On Adoptions

We have been appalled at the number of parents whose adopted children are in rebellion. "Bad seed," one professional expert in the field claims. According to this theory, the parents who gave birth to the child were irresponsible, unstable people and passed these characteristics on to their baby.

In some cases, this might be true. I wonder, however, if we might consider the possibility that the adopted child "rebels" because from the moment he enters his new home, he is told he is different. "You are adopted." I doubt if all the "I chose you" business changes the fact one bit that he is not LIKE other children.

Another consideration is this: A friend who has a rebellious adopted youngster said she felt Christian parents have to be especially cautious for Satan is so disturbed that the child has been snatched from his domain that he attacks the child and the family furiously.

George has handled a number of adoptions and it is his feeling that all three theories might be true in one case or the other. In any event, adoptive parents need to be especially loving, firm and diligent to teach the child God's word. But most of all, they must pray.

DISCIPLINE—WE CAN'T AGREE

What do you consider the best means of discipline for children?

It depends on the child. A spanking by Daddy for one will

straighten him up for weeks. Others respond negatively to a spanking. (Physical punishment is not recommended for teenagers. With them, withholding privileges is best). Reinforcing good behavior should be understood and practiced more by all of us. For instance, if a mother gives her child a graham cracker every time he yelps, whimpers or yowls "Cracker!" she is teaching him that when he wants anything he need only yelp, whimper or yowl. If little Leroy is told to pick up a toy and he shakes his head and goes about his business and the mother sighs, picking it up herself, he will learn that he doesn't ALWAYS have to do what he's told and will soon be resisting almost EVERYTHING he's told. On the other hand, if the mother gives her child a graham cracker when he is being quiet and playing well, he will associate that with quiet play. If he is told to pick up a toy with the promise that, as soon as he does, there will be a new game waiting for him, he will associate obedience with nice things.

Get Together

How do we begin to agree on child rearing philosophies?

Research everything the Bible has to say regarding children. Put it together so you can get a complete picture. Read books by top authors on the subject—you'll find a few listed in our bibliography. Use your common sense. Talk it over together as a couple to see where you agree and where you don't. Work from that angle.

Remember, in case of disagreement, Dad should have the final say (See Chapter Seven "Who's Running This Show Anyway?"). Your disagreements should never be in front of the children who soon learn to divide and conquer.

Train Them To Help

Should children (boys ages 8, 15, and 17) be expected

to help mother vacuum, dust do dishes, etc., when husband NEVER helps?

Of course. Assign them chores and follow through. Remain sweet and loving, explaining to them that:

1) They helped make the mess. They help clean it up.
2) You are teaching them to be thoughtful of others.
3) You are not as strong as they and NEED their muscles.
4) Someday they will be husbands. This will make them GOOD ones.

If they say, "Dad doesn't do it, and he's a good husband," you can say with a twinkle, "One of the reasons why Daddy is such a good husband is because he has such a good wife. You might not be so blessed. Now get going."

Quiet Children?

How can you make three small children quiet down before Daddy comes home? I'm sure their attitudes help set our moods and vise versa.

That's asking an awful lot! The best way is for Dad to come home and get into a good wrestling match with them. But if he has to have his peace and quiet, then perhaps you can plan your day so you have a "reading" time starting just before he enters. Reserve a few books which they seldom see and bring them out for "story time."

Another possibility is (after you've cleaned them up "for Daddy"), separate them and give each a special "WHEN DADDY COMES HOME" box which you have decorated with pretty wrapping paper; a box in which you have put interesting items like plastic jars with lids they can take on and off, a pile of animal pictures in a special box, a box of cupcake papers, a special little book, and other things you can find in any cupboard in the average home. Change the items from time to time and let them exchange boxes now and then.

If you don't start them on this too soon, they should still be going strong by the time Pop walks in the door. Somewhere along the line, try to get a shower, put on perfume and fix your hair for him.

Eat It!

> *Should children be expected to eat everything on their plates?*

One family insisted on this at every meal. The daddy was a big, strong serviceman who didn't dare be challenged, so the children ate. The unreasonable part of it was that the portions doled out to the children were as big as that given to the dad! When they reached their teen years, they both became fatties. It's GOOD to teach children not to waste and most certainly to eat some of EVERYTHING mother cooks without protest, but start them with small portions of each. After they've eaten ALL of that, allow them to have more if they want it.

A little five year-old we know is a problem eater. She eats only what she wants and when she wants it. When she first set her jaw and refused what was offered her at age one, she was allowed to get down from her high chair, go have a romp and then start to bawl because she was hungry. Of course she was fed—something more appealing—a cookie, a cracker— ANYTHING to keep her quiet. Between meal snacks, if they are small, nutritious and not filling, are okay, but not if the meal was refused. After a few minutes, if a child refuses to eat, he or she should be put down and not allowed to have even a drink of milk until the next meal, no matter how much he or she cries. Before long, smart little children will learn that, if they don't want to be painfully hungry, they had better eat what is before them, because Dad and Mom can out-stubborn them every time.

THE SCREAMIN' TEEN

A family with a teenage son couldn't understand why, all of a sudden, he became insufferable. Their other children had not rebelled at all in their teen years, and this child had been treated no differently than they. He started yelling at them, refusing to obey, threatening to run away from home and commit suicide. He had been complaining of severe headaches, but physical examinations revealed nothing. Then he complained because his back felt "tight" and he frequently asked someone to pound on it. On a hunch, his folks took him to a chiropractor. X-rays revealed severe neck injuries with a curvature in the spine resulting from them. Unable to remember any specific accidents, they were told that just getting hit in the head with a basketball, or falling down could have done it. Treatments were begun immediately. Within weeks the headaches started to disappear and his behavior improved considerably. The parents fully expected him to return to normal within a year, for since then they have talked with other people who have experienced the same thing.

An Enemy

Teenagers are ripe for injuries of all sorts because of the active lives they lead. On top of that, we are convinced that the cokes, hamburgers, sweets and other junk food they eat often result in the rebellious behavior we see in so many of them. They are duck soup for all sorts of medical problems including acne.

It's good to start reading some health facts to them (see our Bibliography), explaining that you feel that one of the reasons they are so unhappy at home is because they aren't really well. If you can get them in the habit of taking a 15 minute snooze and eating a HEALTHY snack when they get home, you will be far ahead. Have tempting morsels available for them: fresh fruit drinks, protein drinks, cookies and sweet breads made with whole wheat pastry flour and less sweetening than usual, whole wheat crackers and cheeses which haven't had coloring or preservatives added to them. Nuts and dried fruits are a nice combination. If you can get raw milk from a commercial source, it is far healthier than pasteurized and worth the extra pennies. Let them drink all they will. For teenagers with acne, see if chocolate is the culprit. Withhold it for a period. Try substituting carob (found in health food stores). It's delicious.

Discovering The Opposite Sex

Does a teenage daughter need her daddy's love, so that she doesn't seek young boys' attentions?

When you can stop teenage girls from seeking boys' attentions, you'll be changing the course of human nature. Forget it. The thing you want to do is guide her so her interest is healthy and progresses at a safe rate. Have many friendly talks with her (the best is off-the-cuff while you are cooking or cleaning her closet together). Give her articles and books to read. Point out to her ahead of time the possible problems that may confront her and tell her ways to meet them. No scare tactics.

Teenage girls very definitely need Dad to throw a ball with them, tell them how pretty they are, bring them a gift occasionally, be available to talk to and be firm on what they can and cannot do. Too often dads leave the training of the older girls to the moms, and often with disastrous results. Girls and mothers lock horns more than anyone likes to believe. In the process, mother ages 10 years in two and daughter looks back with regret after she's matured.

Here's Solid Help

Lots of folks have all sorts of exciting things going on to keep your teenager on the right path! Campus Crusade for Christ has training courses for high school and college ages. Youth For

Christ is operating on many high school campuses, Christians have rallies, conferences and concerts for your young people and churches try to have active youth groups to take up the slack in the social life. Get your children involved! If the youth groups are dead, get involved and do something to make them come alive!

Charley "Tremendous" Jones, a popular lecturer, had his own method of keeping his son on the right track, aside from those mentioned above. He paid him $10 for every book he would read that Dad picked out for him. They weren't all religious books, but all were uplifting and character forming. He had to give a written report on the content. The boy made hundreds of dollars and his dad came out the winner.

Guidelines For Dating

Many Christian parents don't allow their children to start dating until they are 16, except for "special" affairs such as the Christmas banquet at church, and then only if the couple goes with several others. When the magic age arrives, they start out with double dates. If the teenager proves trustworthy by getting home on time and keeping within any other guidelines, single dating begins.

Parents should be careful not to make the mistake of assuming that a grown-up person is inside those grown-up teenage bodies. They should have additional responsibilities and be treated like adults as much as possible, but they still need guidance, regarding WHO they date, HOW WELL you know their friends before they date, WHAT they are going to do on the date, and WHEN they are to be home.

When our daughter started to date singly, she was interested in several boys. One who caught her eye for a short time had a reputation around church of being a fast driver and running with a wrong crowd. We told her we liked him, but before she would be allowed to go anywhere with him, we would have to have a talk with him. He was so nervous about it, he couldn't sleep. During the talk, he was polite and honest and explained to our satisfaction how he felt about issues we questioned. He promised not to go over the speed limit (he went *under* all the way) and also promised not to ask to be around her except occasionally until he got his life straightened out. He was a marvelous gentleman on their date, treating her like the princess we always want her to feel she is.

Pray, Pray, Pray

One wise mother formed a group of ladies who meet weekly for one purpose: to pray for their teenagers. Good idea?

DIVORCE DISASTERS

Probably the most convincing argument against divorce is what happens to the children. Any way you cut the pie, children suffer and suffer greatly — far more than the parents who aren't able to get out of themselves long enough to make a contract work.

Redbook magazine reports a study on children of divorced parents. Conducted by a child psychologist and a lecturer on social welfare, the study traced the behavior of 131 children, 110 of whom were under 13, over a period of 4 years. The result of their study is not pretty. The children experienced great pain, changes in personality and behavior, and general undesirable reactions. Some of them did well at first and lapsed into troubled conditions later on. Others did just the reverse. None of the children under 13 wanted the divorce to take place, even when they had witnessed great violence. All the children worried about their own future.

The conclusion of the Redbook report was that divorce is here to stay (they have startling figures to back them up: In 1960 there were 393,000 divorces in this country; by 1974 the figure soared to 970,000) and that it is imperative to find ways to help children weather the ordeal.

We're pleased someone is trying to help these unfortunate victims of domestic war, but we would urge parents to solve the problem by not getting a divorce in the first place. It's one thing for a battered wife to tell a child, "We have gone away from Daddy for awhile so he won't hurt people anymore. When he gets cured of his problem, we will go back," and quite another to say, "We're getting a divorce." Divorce is final. It shatters security. It smashes lives.

Set-Up For Trouble

Because of the unholy rush to the courts, however, many people find themselves confronted with stepchildren. We have had great concern for girls whose mothers remarry. No matter how "in love" they think they might be with the new man, they should move carefully and cautiously. Stepfathers are notorious for molesting stepchildren in their own homes.

At best the situation is less than desirable:

> *My stepchildren make life miserable for me. They are jealous of my relationship with their father. I'm afraid they will break us up. What can I do?*

Ride the storm with love, kindness and firmness. You are an intruder in their family, and they may even be holding you responsible for their mother not being there, true or not. Never speak against their mother. Do fun things with them, and *for* them. Try surprising them (one at a time) by serving them breakfast in bed some morning, with a happily decorated tray. Plan picnics, games and other fun family things. Allow them to dominate Dad's attention part of the time. Take their side sometimes on issues wherever it is possible (never against Daddy). Take time to read to them, share beautiful thoughts with them and lead them spiritually.

If you must punish them, or stand your ground, explain that you love them very much (even if they scream they hate you) and as their "mother" you must do what is best for them, even if it hurts a little. If you have children of your own, be careful you don't treat them more fairly than you do your stepchildren. You'll soon win them over and they will be a blessing to you throughout your life.

> I have a 21 year-old stepson who dropped out of school and who has come back home to live. He has no job. He does no chores around the house, even when I ask him to do so, or offer to pay him. He talked his father into financing him through college against my wishes. I feel that his father is destroying him and the rest of our family (4 other children) by not taking a stand. What is your opinion?

We think you need more love, compassion and understanding. True, it is aggravating to have a big clunk lazying around the house, and it is irritating not to have him finish school! It's hard to want to help someone who won't help himself! But, let's look at a few facts:

1) He was undoubtedly hurt by the loss of his family through divorce (or death). He may even be experiencing guilt.
2) As a result, he is like a ship at sea. He has not found himself.
3) At least he is coming to be near people whom he hopes can help him in some way—like reaching out for a plank when you are drowning. He probably has no one else to whom he can turn.
4) Given love, understanding, time, guidance and lots of praise, he may surprise you and make something of himself.
5) And if you have been a beautiful person, he will always consider you with great fondness.

Ask his father to set up some simple chores for him to do "because he is part of the family team and teams have to work together," just like you have for the younger children. It might be best to give him ones that help his Dad, rather than you. Have your husband follow through on them, not you.

As far as the money for his education is concerned, leave your husband alone. He undoubtedly feels sorrow, too, for what has been done to his son whom he remembers as a sweet, trusting little boy whose world was destroyed. Helping him financially is one way he can say, "I'm sorry."

Do lots of nice little things for him, smile a lot and encourage him to talk.

Do's And Don'ts

One of the most thrilling things about children is their individuality. In every child are the seeds of greatness. Yet, much as we parents recoil at the thought of it, in every child is a potential for evil. It is the parent's job to coax out the greatness and help the child subdue that which will lead him along wrong paths. There is no book written that will cover all problems with which parents have to deal. What works for your neighbor might not work with a single ONE of your brood. On the other hand, they might, so we're offering a few do's and don't's which we have learned either by success or failure. Maybe they can be of help to you:

- Don't make excuses for a child's bad behavior. Deal with it.
- Do follow through on any order you give, after making sure it was understood, allowing reasonable time limits.
- Don't expect children to act like adults. They can't.
- Don't be afraid to use little rewards for good behavior and accomplishment.
- Do teach your children to do things "just for love."
- Do try to ignore some of the unpleasant things your "troublemaker" does. Reserve your criticism and punishment for the more serious infractions.
- Don't let a single untruth go by without making a big deal of it. A child who learns early that it doesn't pay will be able to be trusted later on.

- Do keep your eye on your children. Check on small ones every 5 minutes. Don't leave older ones to play for long periods without checking frequently. Know where your teenagers are at all times if possible. You not only have a right to know what they are doing, you have a responsibility.
- Do allow children to make decisions in areas where parental authority is not an issue.
- Don't allow a child to make decisions that should obviously be yours.
- Do treat handicapped children with as much discipline and firmness as those who are not.
- Don't be afraid to set definite guidelines for your teenagers and stick with them no matter how bullyish or unhappy they get. (For instance, if you don't want rock and roll music in your home, don't allow it.) Be ready to give sound reasons for your decisions.
- When a child cries because he doesn't get his own way, don't rush to make him happy. Let him learn that selfishness causes unhappiness.
- Do try to be loving and kind, even when you must deal with disobedience or disrespect.
- Do try NOT to panic, feel personally hurt and rebuffed, or furious when your children are unbelievably unbelievable.

P.S. from Margaret: Mom, Dad, when you feel your children are just a big pain, remember what George has always said to me: "Don't be upset, honey. The pain will soon be gone." Then, through my tears, I question:

One tiny voice lisping, "Mother . . ."
Sweet tones uplifted in song.
Laughing and playing with her brother;
Heartbreak when something went wrong.

Carefully watching o'er sister,
Putting fish worms in a can.

Trying to be like father
Wanting to prove he's a man.

Now she's a lovely young lady
Throwing a kiss as she goes by.
Handsome and strong he towers o'er us—
Strength and purpose in his eye.

What will they take away with them?—
Memories of sorrow or joy?
Oh, that the past could be lived over
With one little girl and boy.

by Margaret Hardisty

11

Relatives Can Ruin A Marriage

THE GANG-UP

Evidentally, some of it begins in parents' minds because of
doubts like this voiced to us in a seminar:

> *What can you do to help your married children when
> you see them making mistakes?*

They are going to make lots of mistakes before they get to
where you are, just like you did. That's part of the maturing
process. If they are truly headed for disaster, you can open the
door with a few comments to see if they WANT the benefit of
your knowledge. If not, stand aside. If so, offer your advice only
after you have drawn them out to see if you can get them to
think it through themselves.

Stand Up For Right

> *What do you do when your parents encourage your
> children to sin?*

Take your stand on issues you feel are important. If they refuse to heed what you say, then the children will have to be taught that Grandma and Grandpa do not obey God and the children must not do anything they say without asking Mother and Daddy first. If they repeat what you have said to the grandparents, so be it.

A man asked his father not to curse in front of his young son. He didn't want the boy to pick up those words. The father sulked and only the daughter-in-law's pleading kept him from going home immediately. Nothing was ever said about it again, but the little boy never heard curse words from grandpa after that.

They Aren't Friends

Our relatives on both sides cause friction by cutting, unkind remarks, playing favorites with our children, being envious when something good happens to us and getting a good laugh when misfortune strikes. What can we do?

It's a fact of life that you can choose your friends, but you have to take what you get when it comes to relatives. You would be much better off if you lived farther away from them. Cut down on visits and get involved in something else instead: work at the church, hobbies, etc. Just don't be as available to them. Avoid using them for baby-sitters, no matter how tight your budget is.

And why in the world are you sharing your business with them? They don't need to know all of your misfortunes, and if it makes them envious, they don't need to know your good fortune. Blood runs thicker than water? Sometimes the best thing is to be sure there's a river running between you, with a boat available only for occasional use.

Rest Home Round-Up?

What about when our parents get old?

How would you like your children to treat you when you get old? One of the tragedies of our times is the parent who is shut away in a rest home and left there to die. Even husbands and wives do it to each other with the least excuse. It sickens me to go into a beautiful home with lots of room and find out they have mother ''in a rest home.'' They always hasten to say she's happier there. But seldom is that true. Whether it's your mother or dad, just remember who took care of you day and night for many, many years so you could get a good start in life! When you had sickness, they comforted you and helped you get well; when you had accidents, they cleaned them up; when you felt frightened or alone, they loved you. When you couldn't read, they read to you. You owe honor and respect to your parents as long as they're on the earth. If you can afford to put them in a rest home, you can afford to get someone to come into your home to sun them, walk them, bathe them or whatever is necessary so the major part of the work doesn't fall on your shoulders.

If you make them feel part of the family, and yet arrange it so they have their own lives, you will be doing as God has commanded. It will be pleasing to you as well as to them, knowing that you have repaid a bit of the sacrifice they suffered for you.

If they are crochety or ornery, give them lots of vitamins, level with them and put up with it. We know senility can be a problem. That's why you hire someone to help out.

When my handsome, laughing, lovable father became a victim of many small strokes, it finally began to affect his mind. My mother, after some 50 years of marriage, wasn't about to relegate him to an institution. Everyone watched amazed while that frail little woman who had once been the beauty of the countryside where she grew up, faithfully tended her love, even after he got to the point where he no longer knew who she was a good portion of the time. She refused to move in with any of us because she felt that the only thing at all he had left that was familiar to him was his home and she didn't want to remove him from that.

When at last he got to where he could do nothing by himself and she wasn't strong enough to lift him, she consented to putting him in an institution. She couldn't be with him much of the time for several weeks for it was in another city, and within a short time he was gone. If more people showed that kind of devotion, we would have less infirm, heartbroken old people crowding the rest homes where they are pumped full of medicine to keep them quiet.

HIS FOLKS

How can you get your husband to talk to you rather than his folks?

One wife, whenever she and her husband talked things over, insisted loudly and vocally that she was right, on almost any issue that came up. If she was proved to be wrong, she would refuse to back down. Her reactions were immature and showed her insecurity. As a result her husband quit talking with her altogether. Instead he started airing his problems to his mother.

Francine complained about this same problem, but counseling revealed that the cause was her jealousy and possessiveness.

If, after you have honestly evaluated the situation and ascertained that the source of the trouble is you, then change! If it is a problem with your husband, start a patient, loving education program so he can see what he is doing to himself by hanging on to his parent's shirttails.

All young couples should use the advice of their parents

occasionally but in the long run, the decisions have to be theirs and they must be made with finality. If they make mistakes, so what? We learn from mistakes. It's the fellow who never makes mistakes who never gets anything worthwhile done in life.

Improvement Needed

> *My husband's parents can't forgive me for taking away their "baby boy." It has caused trouble.*

Most parents are willing to give up a "baby boy" if they feel they've gained a daughter. If you haven't reached out to them with a great amount of love, going out of your way to let them know you appreciate them and generally making them feel GOOD about you, then the fault may lie in your own heart.

One wife was so possessive of her husband, and determined to let the parents know that he belonged to her now, that she resented their calls, their visits and their questions about the children or their life. These are not healthy emotions. The couple eventually divorced. She bitterly and unfairly blamed his parents for the breakup.

I Want To Be Part Of Them

> *My husband works at his parents' place of business. We are farmers. I'm left alone day after day. I feel left out.*

Then join them for part of each day. Tell them you want a job too. Or if you can't do that, drive over during the week with a picnic lunch to share with them, or just with him. If you have sewing or ironing, perhaps your mother-in-law wouldn't mind if you did it at her house, "because I get so lonesome for everyone." When you and your husband are home alone, make it a fun, happy time, so he'll be eager to get home more quickly.

Thoughtless Remarks

> *His folks rib me about not having more than one child. I've lost three and it hurts a lot.*

They probably think they're helping to ease the pain by making light of it. And maybe you're allowing yourself to be too sensitive. If you can't cope, however, ask your husband to talk with them. If he won't, then you must—kindly and sweetly.

The Big Boss

> *My father-in-law is always giving me orders. And my husband does nothing about it. This is causing much tension.*

When I was pregnant with my daughter, we visited my husband's uncle. He kept telling me to sit down. Everytime I'd move, he'd say, "Sit down, honey." Ten thousand times on that weekend he told me to "Sit down, honey," until I thought I'd never want to sit down again! If we had lived near him, I would have completely avoided him until my baby was born.

With a father-in-law who is close by, it's different, although his motives may be the same. He probably considers you a sweet, pretty little thing that doesn't know enough to come in out of the rain. Therefore he is doing you a kind turn by setting things in order. You'll have to take your stand. When he orders you to do something you don't care to do, simply say, "Dad, that particular thing is not on my list for today," throw him a kiss and leave the room to busy yourself doing something else.

HER FOLKS

> *My wife's relatives are always getting into big confabs, arguing and fussing, and invariably they draw my wife*

into them. This upsets her and me, too. What can we do?

Personal story coming up. Both of us came from arguing families. We grew up in an atmosphere that sizzled hotter than the turkey on the Thanksgiving Day we had all gathered to celebrate. The crazy thing about it was that some of them would be arguing one side of a question vehemently, and then, all of a sudden, they would change and take opposite sides and argue it as surely as they had the first position. We kept wishing that dinner would be called before someone broke all tradition and blacked another guy's eye.

We both agreed that we didn't want that in our lives, although we had learned to argue right along with the best of them. Calm, intelligent discussions were much more appealing and not nearly as hard on the constitution, or digestion.

If you have those kind of relatives and it bothers you when they start in, change the subject, or leave the room. If they drag you into the debate by telephone, have an excuse to hang up or tell them you'll think about it, allow yourself one minute to think about it after you hang up, and then forget it. Don't call them back, give your opinion or become part of it unless it involves you directly and action has to be taken.

Pandering Pals

My folks are always asking for handouts. It embarrasses me. I want my husband to respect them but how can he?

We are to honor our parents until they die, and there are times of emergency when you should be willing to help them financially. But just as a husband mustn't give in to his wife's every whim because it wouldn't be good for her, so you mustn't supply their every want. If they haven't learned to stand on their own two feet by now, they should have. Just simply tell them you have nothing you can give them at the time.

If they are truly in need, try to help them work out a plan where they can save and budget (see Chapter 5, Money! Money! Money!) and help themselves become self-supporting. If all else fails, find part-time work for them where they can earn a few dollars for those extras.

Get A New Partner

> *My father took advantage of us in a business partner-ship. My husband kept quiet because I was torn be-tween not wanting to hurt my father and saving my husband the loss. It has caused tension.*

If it is over and done with, it is water under the bridge. Forget and forgive. But avoid any business dealings with Papa in the future.

THE MOTHER-IN-LAW

It seems as if mothers compete for the position of NO. 1 CULPRIT in making the lives of married children miserable. We seldom see it happen in a family where the mother has been supplied with lots of romance and attention by her husband. When she isn't, she reaches out in any way she can to supply her own, and the results are sometimes disastrous. She'll try to hang on to a daughter, unconsciously becoming a wedge between her and her husband. She'll desire to continue to be the main woman in her son's life, thus alienating his wife. Thus we have a question that speaks for many young people:

> *How do you handle a mother who does not want to cut the apron strings and constantly interferes in our marriage?*

Some couples have moved to another city. It works fine, unless Mother follows them.

Others have introduced their mother to several men and women her age, hoping to get her interested in something besides them. That works sometimes, although it's harder if she has moved in with you.

Others encourage Mother to start baby or house sitting for friends of theirs. When she works, she has less time to be a bother.

As a last resort, others talk it over together, decide what Mother should be allowed to be part of and what she shouldn't. Then they talk with her explaining how they feel. Sometimes she gets insulted, hurt, threatens to have a heart attack and all sorts of things, and often tries to continue right on interfering in their lives. But sometimes it's the only way to go and it is effective.

Whatever course you take, stick with it as long as it works. Then try something else.

Your life is your own. Mother should be allowed to visit occasionally and you should make a point of inviting her for an evening once in awhile, but the in-and-out everyday lady is too much for anyone to take. Resist talking over your problems in her presence or sharing with her if she tends to take over. If she complains because "you didn't tell me" explain why.

> *How do you handle a mother-in-law who always finds fault with anything you do? How do you handle visits that are usually on the tense note? Especially as the holidays approach!*

How many mother-in-law jokes have you heard? Like ethnic jokes, they can color your thinking so that you don't see things accurately, and the least little thing mother-in-law does is interpreted as a nasty.

However, if things are as you say, then your next step is to be patient, loving and kind to Mother and when she criticizes, ignore her, change the subject and give her something to do which will make her feel useful.

If there is tension in the visits, it's probably because you're taking things too seriously. Be glad to see her, let her know that sincerely, hug her lovingly, whirl her around, have the children primed with things to show her and games to play with her. Keep her so busy and happy she hasn't time to do anything but enjoy it.

QUIZ FOR RELATIVES

Answer yes or no. Check your score at the bottom.
1. Do you insist your children (or brother or sister) see you often?
2. When they choose otherwise, do you take it as a personal affront?
3. Do you drop in unexpectedly fairly often?
4. Do you give lots of advice when they ask for it (or when they don't)?
5. Do you let them know when they aren't rearing their children properly?
6. Do you probe for their family secrets?
7. Do you take sides when they quarrel?
8. Do you let one of them take shelter with you when they quarrel?
9. Do you telephone them more than twice a week, normally?
10. Do you let them struggle through their financial needs or goals without your help, most of the time?
11. Do you write them frequently, assuming you live at a distance?
12. Do you have an active, productive life of your own, not wrapped around them?
13. Do you seek friends other than your relatives?
14. Are you financially independent of them?
15. Do you accept your children's mates with love and ZERO criticism?
16. If there is a family business, do you allow all the family to have a voice in running things?

17. Are you the kind of relative they can brag about to their friends?

If you answered "Yes" to Questions 1-9 and "No" to Questions 10-17, you need to reverse the trend and go the other direction. You are making life difficult for them.

P.S. from George: Don't be too anxious to be free of your loved ones. Enjoy them. You and they might need each other some day.

12

Almost Too Much To Bear

THE GYRATING GIANT—IMMATURITY

Occasionally someone will come out with a list of qualities which are supposed to be marks of a mature person. It's rather like the fellow who writes a book on "How To Be Humble." It seems to me that the only truly mature person who ever walked the earth was the Lord Jesus Christ. The rest of us have too many inconsistencies in our nature, too much ego to battle, too much finger-pointing at the other fellow. Actually, we've been dealing with immaturity since the beginning chapter, but there are some things that stick out and make living with a person a pain in the neck from the toe up.

My wife is totally self-centered. She has to be gratified at all costs.

Is she getting lots of small attentions from you? If not, it's time to fill her daily Christmas stocking starting today. On the other hand, she might be spoiled. As you supply her emotional needs, keep in mind that some things aren't good for her—always having her own way, for instance. You must refuse at times, but do so kindly, explaining why.

Easily Offended

Here's an all too common problem:

My husband is the type who takes offense if I bring something to his attention.

Learning to take criticism is a mark of maturity. The more self-centered a person, the quicker he is to let his hackles rise. I used to think that being unable to take criticism came from insecurity. I still believe it, but my definition of "insecurity" has changed. There are those born who want their world to be just the way they want it, and woe unto anyone who tries to change it. Any suggestion that things aren't quite as they should be is met with indignation. All criticism is taken as a personal affront. There is a need to defend oneself at all costs even if it is proved to everyone else's satisfaction that the recipient is wrong.

A person like this needs to get it through his or her thick head that criticism can be a tremendous HELP! Without a doubt, some criticism is given in ignorance, or is misplaced, and some is just meant to hurt. All criticism, however, should be analyzed calmly, with the old mental spyglass, and if it has value, it should be taken seriously. Once a person gets to that point, he finds it a great relief not to have to defend his kingdom any longer.

Put Him Down

And now a different angle:

What makes a man put down most things around him? How can he be led to joy?

Sometimes I think there should be a national club for "Put-Downers." They could meet monthly to "put-down" to their hearts' content and vote on who was master of the art, so those at home would get a rest. They are miserable people to have around.

One fellow I know tromps on anything and everybody to anybody who'll listen! His parents did it all wrong, this person insulted him, that person's jokes were meant to knife him, the choir director is inept, the pastor really stepped out of line today. When he feels complimentary, rather than coming right out with it he hides his compliments in "constructive criticism." He's so in the habit of being negative that he doesn't even know he's doing it. Nor can it be pointed out to him, unless the "pointer-outer" wants to be put on his list to receive the choicest put-downs whenever he shows his face, and sometimes when he doesn't.

Your man needs professional help to find out why he feels so insecure (in many cases, knocking others makes the knocker feel superior). He also needs a close walk with God. A song we first heard at a Billy Graham Crusade says it nicely:

> "Take a look at yourself and you will look at others differently
> By putting your hand in the hand of the man from Galilee."[5]

If you are the unfortunate one to live with a "putter-downer," discourage his weakness by not responding to his gossip. Change the subject to something happy. Teach your children, in front of him, that if they can't say nice things about other people, say nothing at all, and then insist on that rule.

> *When my husband and I are going to have a quiet evening or time alone, it is always up to me to make it enjoyable. Can't cope. It always falls through.*

---

5. Words and music by Gene MacLellan, *Put Your Hand In The Hand*, Beechwood Music of Canada, Don Mills (Ontario, Canada, 1970). All U.S. rights assigned Beechwood Music Corp. Used by special permission.

Plan ahead. Have several fun things ready to go. If one doesn't work, you can fall back on another. Ask him to plan a time together occasionally. Learn to laugh, and not take life so seriously.

The Not So Jolly Green Giant

I'm jealous of my wife. There's no reason for it. I know I'm going to lose her if I don't quit.

Jealousy is not love. It's possessiveness. It's fear. It's hanging onto the pacifier long past time. You need to fill your mind full of beautiful things so there won't be time for you to ruminate on "possibilities." There is a passage of scripture that might help you. It comes from the greatest psychiatrist ever:

"Whatever things are true, whatever things are honest, whatever things are just, whatever things are pure, whatever things are lovely, whatever things are of good report, if there be any virtue, and if there be any praise, think on these things."

Another favorite of ours is:

"Casting down imaginations, and every high thing that exalteth itself against the knowledge of God, and bringing into captivity every thought to the obedience of Christ."

ALCOHOL—SCOURGE OF HUMANITY

Many people have asked us about alcoholism. There is little hope for someone who refuses to seek help but there have been many success stories for those who do. One wrote:

It was years before both of us faced up to the fact that alcohol was our problem. We blamed everything else. Finally, we realized it was a disease and went for help.

If thinking alcoholism is a disease gets you out for help, then keep thinking it. That's the popular way of putting it, so no one feels guilty. But alcoholism is attributable to a force bigger than yourself having hold of you, and we feel that force is evil, with sin as the result. If you admit alcoholism is sin, and surrender your life to the Lord Jesus Christ, you will see a miracle take place. (See Chapter Fourteen, God and You). Becoming religious and a church-goer doesn't do it. It's the personal relationship with God that counts. Then your cure is permanent.

A man we knew well, an alcoholic and a disc jockey, was befriended by a preacher. Through the years, the man of the cloth never gave up. On the day the imbiber received Christ, he walked by a bar, got a whiff of alcohol and threw up. He never needed a drink after that. That's God's power.

But if you aren't willing to go that route, get help from organizations which are set up for helping people with this problem. They can be effective.

The Mean Drunk

My husband abuses me when he drinks. What can I do?

One woman we know put up with it for some years, and finally filed for divorce. Her husband, in his grief, wandered into a church, found the Lord, and has never drunk since. Their marriage has become a heaven on earth compared to their former life. Although we don't recommend filing for divorce, we do have some suggestions, coming up in the next part of this chapter.

The Lover

> *Sex? He falls asleep before we begin.*

That's no surprise. Alcohol inhibits the liver from breaking down estrogen which in turn builds up in the body and takes away the sex drive of male and female.

Where Does It All Begin?

We are convinced that most of it begins with "social drinking." Every alcoholic we've talked with took his first drink under the watchful eye of his parents who were teaching him to handle it "properly." We know of hundreds of families who won't have alcohol in their home. They entertain lavishly and successfully without it.

As far as we've been able to see, nothing good comes from alcohol. Many people who cheat on their mates wouldn't do so without a few drinks under their belts. Our government leaders make delicate decisions which affect the safety of our lives while their brains are dulled by the sauce. There would be untold numbers of children who would have food and clothing if it weren't for drinking parents. As for us and our house—no thanks!

PHYSICAL AND MENTAL ABUSE

> *My husband takes my kindness and gentleness to be a weakness and proceeds even more flagrantly to trample my feelings and ignore me. What should be my response?*

Become stronger. Don't allow your vulnerable spots to show. These kind of men sometimes marry just to have someone on whom they can take out their meanness. They enjoy cruelty. Don't give him a chance. Start standing up for your rights (be sure they are reasonable), not crudely, nor loudly, but firmly, and follow through on them. Allowing a man like this to continue to hurt you causes him to become even worse and you are doing him more harm than good, as well as yourself.

Same Song, Second Verse

Too many women have asked questions similar to the following:

> *My husband beats me. I just got out of ten days in the hospital from his kicking me. He's always sorry, he says. I love him. I should go back to him, shouldn't I?*

First, you will have to face up to an important question honestly. Do you enjoy being beaten? If so, you need intensive counseling from a professional. If not, then the answer is NO. You are encouraging his weakness by standing around being a punching bag for the big baby. Go where he can't find you. If you have to quit your job and get another to do that, do it. If you have children, take them with you, or he'll start practicing his punches on them. Keep in touch by letter and phone, encouraging him to get help and promising to return when he's cured. Of course you take the chance of his getting a divorce, and that's one of the reasons why punching bags are afraid to yell quits. But very likely, especially if he tells you he loves you at other times, he will get help and shape up. You can even send him the name and address of people who can straighten him out; a minister, a psychologist, or an organization.

> *How should a wife react when a husband praises her in public but also belittles and puts her down.?*

Be patient and smiling in public. Everyone around will be laughing on the outside, but on the inside they will be down on him and sympathetic with you. When you are alone with him, have a frank talk, pointing out exactly what he said and why it was humiliating to you.

> *My husband continues to laugh at something that hurt me long ago.*

He may mean no harm over it, even though it is unkind of him to do it. Why don't you try to see the funny side of it, if he ignores your request not to bring it up again? Carrying a grudge hurts the carrier more than the other guy.

> *Both of us lack trust in the other. This has caused trouble in our marriage.*

Analyze why you can't trust. Did it come from your childhood? Talk it over thoroughly. Both of you should try not to do anything that would cause the other to have suspicions. Then, when either of you gets a negative thought or starts drumming up trouble in your mind, force those thoughts out with positive, beautiful thoughts.

P.S. from Margaret: Little wife, if you stand still for abuse, you must have a very low opinion of yourself. You were made in the image of God, not a night crawler. Stand up and be counted!

13

When Love,
Trust or Respect Has Gone

IS DIVORCE THE ANSWER?

Communication is zilch, wounds are deep, scars are thick. Is there any answer besides divorce? George has handled hundreds of divorce cases. He says that in most instances, it could have been prevented. Generally, after the divorce is finalized, both mates go through terrific agony. Divorce solves fewer problems than it creates, and the divorced parties generally carry the same undesirable traits into the next marriage as they had in the last. On top of that, they have to cope with the new person's problems. Their only advantage is that, hopefully, they have grown up a little since the divorce and will try harder in the next union.

But that doesn't help the children. The children suffer far worse agonies than their parents but for them it's too late (see Children Can Be a Pain—Chapter Ten). There are solutions, but you have to WANT to find them and it must begin with your shutting out divorce as a consideration.

What do you recommend for a marriage when love is gone, perpetual animosity reigns, interest in the "estate" is about gone, and only one is born again? Children are involved.

192/HONEST QUESTIONS—HONEST ANSWERS

Born again, yes, but a baby spiritually. One of you has to make the first move toward mending the relationship. As a child of God, you need to be that one. And it will have to start with a desire to please God, instead of yourself. We suggest you look carefully at John 15 and dwell long on . . . .

Verses 1, 2: A SOLEMN WARNING (Jesus speaking)

> "I am the true vine, and My Father is the vinedresser. Every branch in Me that does not bear fruit, He takes away; and every branch that bears fruit, He prunes it, that it may bear more fruit."

(No fruit? God takes away the offender through death, sickness or just not using him or her. Compare with Verse 6 in your Bible.)

Of course, most of us bear SOME fruit, so Verse 2 also contains a reminder: God allows trouble in our lives so we can SEE where we need to grow spiritually.

Verse 4: A COMMAND

> "Abide in Me, and I in you. As the branch cannot bear fruit of itself, unless it abides in the vine, so neither can you, unless you abide in Me."

(Abide? You "abide" in your home. You are continually in it. Let Him envelope your life, too.)

Verse 5: PROMISE

> "I am the vine, you are the branches; he who abides in Me, and I in him, he bears much fruit; for apart from Me you can do nothing."

Verse 7: BIG PROMISE

> "If you abide in Me, and My Words (the Bible) abide in you, ask whatever you wish, and it shall be done for you."

(It's also a big challenge! But just think! It's possible or He wouldn't have dangled it before your hungry eyes. You can see now why your prayers haven't always been answered, can't you?)

Verse 8 : STATEMENT OF FACT

"By this is My Father glorified, that you bear much fruit, and so prove to be My disciples."

(And here all along we thought we were glorifying God in our lives by all the neat service we do. Why, we haven't even learned what the word "discipleship" means!)

Verse 11 : REWARD

"These things I have spoken to you, that My joy may be in you, and that your joy may be made full."

'Nuff said.

But we can't bear much fruit unless we know what fruit is!

Definition Coming Up!

". . . the fruit of the Spirit is love, joy, peace, patience, kindness, goodness, faithfulness, gentleness, self-control . . ."

Is that the kind of fruit you are bearing toward your husband or wife?

HOW TO WIN YOUR WIFE BACK

Remember when you began to fall in love with her—way back when? Remember the flowers you gave her before you took her to the dinner that you worked all day to pay for? Remember when you whispered, "You look so pretty?" Then there were the many phone calls and your mother feared, on the one hand, that you would scrub your skin right off because of the numerous baths you took and rejoiced on the other hand, that at last you combed your hair, remembered to wear deodorant, and put on clean socks?

About the time you started to fall in love with your future wife, she was having to deal with flip-flops in her stomach, too. You began to form in her thinking as the knight in shining armor on a spotless white horse who was going to make all her dreams come true. And you sort of did, for awhile, until after you married her. Then you kept falling off your horse, and your armor got all dented and dirty and you refused to get it hammered out or cleaned, and when she suggested riding lessons, you got peeved. Remember?

Her dreams began to fade, and disillusionment started creeping in. In her frustration and confusion, she began to lash out—at you! Her prince! You lashed back. Later her confusion and anger turned to resentment and then troubles did begin. In the bedroom, for instance. The spontaneous giving of herself to you was all gone.

You're a logical two-plus-two equals four male, aren't you? All right, what is the logical thing to do? TURN BACK THE CLOCK! Impossible? No, it isn't. You can pick yourself up off the ground, register for riding lessons, get your armor pounded into shape and scrub it until it shines like silver!

TO BE PERFECTLY PRACTICAL . . .

1. DON'T get in a HURRY. She needs time to think, to try her wings, to get lonely. Right now, she doesn't want to see your face or hear your voice. A woman who has taken months or years to turn off won't turn on in a week.

   Think in terms of six months to a year. Yes, you *can* go without sexual gratification if you have to. The secret is filling your mind so full of good and creative things that you don't dwell on that need. (No other women, sexually. If she hears about it, your problems will multiply.)

2. GET YOUR LIFE STRAIGHTENED OUT.
   A. Make a list of all the things about you that need to change. Determine to change them.
   B. Next, make your peace with God and start to obey Him. (See Chapter Fourteen—God And You.)

3. IF THERE ARE CHILDREN: Keep frequent contact with them—seeing them, writing notes, occasional gifts. Pick them up at a relative's. If you must pick them up at their home, and she is there, avoid deep conversations, be cheerful, arrive when you say you will and get them back on schedule. Always check ahead to see when is the best time for getting them.

4. KEEP CONSISTENT CONTACT with your wife but not in person. Absence, in your case, makes the heart grow fonder.

At this point, you are going to use your *magnificent male mind* to turn her emotional weakness to your advantage (and ultimately to hers).

1st week: Send a beautiful bouquet of flowers with a simple note such as "These remind me of you." Sign your name. Nothing else.

2nd week: Send a letter sharing something special God has given you. Be sure it doesn't point to any of *her* faults. For instance,

> "The sun was coming up when I read something in my Bible that gave me a great feeling. Maybe God is showing me He loves me. I need to know that right now (This will appeal to her maternal feelings). Anyway, I just wanted to share it with you. Don't ask me why. Maybe it's because I still love you. Maybe it's because you always seemed to understand when I had special thoughts. (This appeals to her because she always knew she was more understanding than you anyway.)

	Then write down what you're talking about! Sign your name.
CAUTION:	Don't copy my note verbatim. If she should read this book and find your notes weren't original, she wouldn't like it!
3rd week:	Send her my book FOREVER MY LOVE, or someone else's book with a note: "Wow, did I ever do a lot of things wrong! I can see now why you were turned off. This book explains a lot of things to me that you were trying to say all along. Please forgive me for hurting you so much." Sign name. Be sure to keep a copy of the book for yourself. Read it several times. Fix these truths in your mind.
4th week:	Send a gift: a small, exquisite necklace, a little crystal dish, a music box, a lovely vase, or something similar. Attach a note: "I couldn't resist this. It's beauty reminds me of you."
5th week:	Write another short letter, sharing something lovely you have seen or heard: A bird? A poem you read? Music?
6th week:	Flowers again!
7th week:	Send cassette tape, if she has a recorder. Put some fun things on it for the kids, then share a Bible devotion with her. At the end, simply say, "I love you."
8th week:	Another book, perhaps, or another gift.

Are you getting the idea? Keep it up! Continue to surprise her by NOT calling or showing your nose.

IN CASE SHE RESPONDS: (This could happen anywhere along the way)

> *If it is negative*, ask her to please keep open. You can say that you don't know what the future holds, but you are seeking God's will, and would she be willing to do that with you?

> *If it is positive*, call her a couple of times to talk, just to see if you can stay on happy subjects. If all goes well, ask her for a date. Move slowly if she accepts. One fellow went against my advice in this matter and went with his wife overnight to a resort spot. He wasn't ready to handle it, *communication*-wise. When he returned, he called and I asked, "How did it go?" He was discouraged. "Terrible," he replied, so we had to start all over again.

ONCE THE DATING BEGINS: Take her to the most atmospheric restaurant you know. Present her with a wristband of flowers. Help her with her coat, her chair and all doors.

> Be fun. Laugh. Be handsome. Assured. Be friendly to those around you—men and women. But keep your focal point on her.

> Every now and then, look sober, search her eyes, and then maybe reach over and squeeze her hand gently. Or wink at her with a little smile. Have a number of subjects ready for discussion. Avoid conversation about your relationship as much as possible.

WHEN YOU TAKE HER HOME: No physical contact, even if she suggests it. Maybe you can take her hand while you walk her to the door. Much as you desire her, you want her to *really* desire you. If you move too soon, she will throw up her defenses.

Call her next time after you've picked up some tickets to a stage play or something cultural. If she refuses, don't ask "Why?" Just wait a little longer before you call her again.

ADDITIONAL IDEAS FOR DATES

Picnics (one with the kids—one without—you supply food)

Boating

Evangelistic meeting

Church social

Kite-flying—or a hike

Window shopping

Horseback riding

Movie (Avoid sexy ones. She'll be suspicious of your intentions.)

Lunch at a nice place

Symphony

Art museum

Opera

After you win her back, what are you going to do? Of course. Go right through the list again—and again—and again!

WHAT ABOUT THE OTHER WOMAN—OR MAN?

If either of you are toying with the idea of having an affair, consider these thoughts:

• Affairs are usually short-lived because they fall into the same problems that marriages do, after you get used to the other person. Meanwhile it may have cost you your marriage, your fortune, your reputation and the respect of your children.

• Affairs usually occur because of chemistry! You are attracted to the other person because of the ZING you've been missing for a long time. You like being with the ZINGER because of what you can GET. It is the lowest form of love and has very little basis for a lasting relationship.

• With your mate, at least you have chalked up some precious memories and shared a lot together. With a little switch in your thinking and actions toward one another, you can build much higher on that foundation and move up to a love that will fulfill all your desires.

> *We've been married for 44 years. My husband was seeing another woman but tells me now he doesn't know why he did. He still loves me, he says. Is it possible for him to feel that way?*

Yes, he can love you and feel an attraction for someone else, all at the same time. The Bible calls it:

> ". . . the lust of the flesh, and the lust of the eyes, and the pride of life . . . ."

Encourage your husband to supply your emotional needs. Then respond to him in submission and love. Both of you get involved in some new and interesting activities. It's never too late to set goals you want to reach. It'll keep him too busy to slip again and make you more fascinating to him.

One little white-haired lady told George, as her husband stood dotingly by her side, "I keep Russ so busy at home he isn't able to stray." She was 80 and he was 86. They've been married 57 years.

If you are having trouble forgiving an errant mate and you are a Christian, take comfort in the fact that God has forgiven you and just think of all the sins you've committed against Him!

HE'S LEFT ME. WHAT DO I DO NOW?

At every seminar, after every lecture, we are approached by

several women with this problem. Women are at a disadvantage because, typically, the male doesn't WANT to be pursued, so she can't inundate him with flowers, love notes, inspirational sharings (he usually sends them back with a "No, thanks") or ask him out on a date.

If your husband has left you, you have to take a different tack.

1. Face up to the fact that, although we have known of cases where the husband left and then came back, they are few compared to those who don't.
2. Straighten out your life spiritually. (See Chapter Fourteen— God And You.)
3. Take stock. Where do your abilities lie? In what direction do your interests move? Start to carve out a new life for yourself and your children.
4. Take a charm course, learn beauty hints, do all the things with your wardrobe, makeup and hair that you should have done while your husband was still home.
5. Prepare for a new career that will bring in higher income.
6. If you meet a new man, be careful. It wouldn't even be a bad idea to have him checked out by a discreet detective, if you entertain serious thoughts about him.
7. If your husband or ex-husband should be in touch with you over business matters or whatever:
   - show no negative emotions (bitterness, iciness, hurt, tears) even if he brings along the girlfriend.
   - be bursting with life and happiness. He'll wonder what's gotten into you.
   - if he asks, just tell him that you can see all the things you did wrong while you were with him and you are changing!
   - if he comes back, receive him with joy (no making him feel guilty, no talking over past grievances or the other woman, no negatives.)
   - be sexier than you ever were with him before he left. Continue your new YOU.

My husband left 10 years ago and never divorced me. He has remarried a woman and had 5 children. What should I do?

Your husband is a bigamist. Your marriage is still valid. But he's not about to come back. Have him get a divorce and forget about him. He can then remarry the woman he now lives with and validate that relationship which is best for the sake of the children.

You should be thankful you can be free of this irresponsible and adulterous man.

How can I forgive the woman who broke up my marriage?

George recalls one woman who sat in his office after her husband ran off with someone else. She aged almost before his eyes as the divorce proceeded. She became lined, bitter and exhibited some ugly characteristics that he would rather not have had around.

Another woman he recalls whose husband left her, radiated with beauty, though her eyes filled with tears now and again. She had decided not to let the knife twist around in her organs. She immediately began to rebuild her life with new friends, new interests, and doing fun things with the children. He saw her bloom despite the ache in her heart. The choice is yours.

My husband fell in love with another woman and divorced me. Now he wants me back. What should I do?

Be careful. Accept his attentions just as you would any other potential mate. Date for months, or even a year or more, so you can observe whether or not he has really matured or not. Educate him kindly on your emotional needs, and make sure he understands that you not only expect these things to be done now, but to continue, should you marry him again.

Chin Up!

While we were on tour recently, we had the privilege of staying in the home of a woman whose husband walked out and now is planning to marry a former schoolmate of hers. We were blessed beyond measure. She had decided that she would not let what happened destroy her. She not only was bustling with things to do, but her home was being used by various groups as a meeting place, including a group of pastors who met there for prayer once a week. She was renting one part of her house to two college-age girls who needed someone to care about them. She counsels women who have had the sorrow of what she went through as well as men, women and young people on every other problem imaginable.

If it worked for her, it can work for you.

14

God And You

THE UNAVOIDABLE FACT

Marriage without God has a much less chance of surviving and remaining hale and hearty than one where Jesus Christ is honored. Despite the fact that Christians have troubles, and we are seeing more Christian marriages dissolving now than ever before, they still are far ahead of their secular counterparts, who would rather do it their own way.

The weakness in Christian marriages seem to fall basically into two camps:

1. A failure of the Christian to mature spiritually.
2. A mixed marriage; one where one partner is born again and the other is not.

In our society where pornography, adultery and lack of character building is accepted as normal, the weak or unequally yoked Christian is walking a dangerous tightrope and too often falls off.

Since the Hardistys have lived on both sides of the fence and have experienced the advantages and drawbacks of both, we say without hesitation, that the person who goes it alone without God is like a man rowing a tiny boat in a tidal wave.

In no way do we wish to hold out to you a picture of us as people who think they've arrived! We struggle with sins and shortcomings that must continually be taken before God for forgiveness. I'm certain that sometimes I hear His venerated voice saying, "Oh, no, here she comes again."

But we discovered long ago that search for wealth, power and pleasure lead to a dead-end in more ways than one! We have chosen rather to follow Him where the pleasures are as delightful as discovering the first wild flowers of spring in a mountain dell. We have decided to let Him lead us until we can go no further. We hold in our hearts His promise and assurance that when our work is done He will carry us into a new land where the fountain of youth flows continuously, where the pain and sorrow that comes from being in a world dominated by hate, greed, fear and a host of ever present evils will never again be seen or experienced. We read with excitement the promise that comes from the very heart of heaven:

> *"Eye hath not seen, nor ear heard, neither have entered into the heart of man, the things which God hath prepared for them that love Him."*

On our journey, we stumble a lot and sometimes slip into the muck by the wayside, but He gently helps us to our feet again, with hands marred by nailprints, and assures us that though the way is not easy, neither is it long, and we will be amply rewarded for any effort we make.

It has been like discovering a huge treasure, rich enough to make the greediest of pirates content! And we would be the greediest of all and the most selfish if we didn't try to share that treasure with others who are groping along trying to find the Way.

We would be hypocrites if we didn't point out the very words of Jesus that seem to jump off the page like sunshine on a brass plate:

> *"I am the way, the truth and the life: no man cometh unto the Father, but by me."*

And—

> "*Come unto Me, all ye that labor and are heavy laden, and I will give you rest. Take My yoke upon you, and learn of Me; for I am meek and lowly in heart, and ye shall find rest unto your souls. For My yoke is easy, and My burden is light.*"

We would be short-sighted if we didn't share with you the fact that God loves you so deeply that He sacrificed His only Son to pay the ransom that will let you out of the prison of self and sin in which the enemy has you locked. Whether you stay in there or not is your choice. Jesus is ready to open the door and lead you to freedom, joy, peace of heart and mind and eternal life the minute you realize your helplessness and cry out to Him.

What would you say to Him if suddenly you were called today to stand before Him? Would you say, "I've done my best," or "I sang in the choir and made soup for my neighbor when she was sick," or "I gave much of my money to charity"? If you did, you'd soon feel very uncomfortable for you would have arrived at the train without your ticket! Your fare to heaven must be paid by the Lord Jesus Christ who shed His blood to buy it for you. When you turn over your life to Him you are handed your ticket and He will never take it away from you again.

> ". . . these have been written that you may believe that Jesus is the Christ, the Son of God; and that believing you may have life in His name."

> "These things I have written to you who believe in the name of the Son of God, in order that you may know that you have eternal life."

It's no thing to be taken lightly. It means the difference between life and death. How about it? He's just a prayer away.

FATHER—THE APPOINTEE

After people break the hold Satan has on them by receiving Christ, God points out to them His Plan for their lives, including what they do in their family relationships. And guess who He has decided is to keep the ball rolling at home as far as spiritual things are concerned? You've got it. The father.

Men have been given such huge responsibilities by God that sometimes they want to hide under the nearest bush and hope He'll pass on to someone else. But our Heavenly Father never calls anyone to a work for which He hasn't equipped him. One of the most sacred duties He has assigned to the father is to be the spiritual head of the home. Many wails reach our ears stating that just the contrary is happening—like this one from a man who has just seen the light:

> Is there any hope for a husband who has never done so to assume leadership in spiritual matters at home?

And some women finally ask in exasperation:

> Since my husband won't take the lead spiritually in our home, should I, or should I just stay quiet and pray?

Being the spiritual head of the family doesn't necessarily mean that Dad has to be the only one to read the Bible aloud, plan the devotions and lead the discussions. It doesn't mean he has to crack the whip and insist on systematic, regular "let's-all-sit-down-now-and-be-quiet-for-our-devotions" type of thing. It does mean that he makes sure SOMEONE in the family is getting spiritual truths across to the children everyday, and we would like to think it would be he, part of the time. Whether it be through learning songs, memorizing verses as a family, or playing games where everyone has to know a verse or Bible story, he or his wife can make spiritual lessons fun. He might seriously consider putting his children in Christian schools so his job will be easier. Praying, reading Christian books together, talking about missionaries and their work, attending church and making sure his children have Christian friends would all certainly fall into his realm of responsibility.

Being a spiritual head means that books, record albums, radio and T.V. programs which might be a detriment to the spiritual life of the household should be ruled out by Dad. IT ALSO MEANS that as the children grow older, Dad may have to change the forms of worship. And most certainly Pop will want to freely, honestly and objectively discuss all issues with his children as they come up: sex, drugs, other religions, politics, crime, etc. Once again, in all these things, Dear Dad doesn't have to be the ONLY one to do it, and, indeed, should be aided right along the way by Mom. Most of all, he should make sure that HE is ACTING AND REACTING spiritually in his home, for children learn much by example.

If he hasn't discovered the JOYS of being God's appointee in the home, then of course, the wife should keep the spiritual fires burning. Many a godly man or woman has looked back and attributed his or her spiritual growth to the determination of a little woman whom they called "Mother."

WHEN ONLY ONE IS BORN AGAIN

Typical of many questions we receive are these:

> *I am a Christian. My husband is not. How do I help him get rid of the rotten books, etc.?*
>
> *How can I keep my non-Christian husband happy and coming home?*
>
> *Should a wife insist on going to church when her husband won't go? What about giving to Christian work?*

Everyone decorates his house differently. We can't give you, and the dozens of others who have pleaded with us for answers, any definite, foolproof formula but we can suggest:

1. First, be sure you are living right. (See Chapter Thirteen, Is Divorce The Answer, for scriptural guidelines.)
2. Stay very close to God with much Bible study and prayer.
3. Be God's kind of wife (See Chapter Two, A Woman Is What A Man Does, and Seven, Who's Running This Show Anyway?).
4. Pray daily for your husband, believing that he will be saved.

Bill Bright, founder and president of Campus Crusade for Christ once told us that he has had the joy of seeing many of his relatives come to Christ. He prayed for each of them in earnest, and then he started praising God for their salvation. Every time he thought of them, he would just thank God that He was going to save them.

We shared this once with a friend who was in despair because none of her husband's relatives had come to Christ even though they had been sending them materials and praying for them for several years. After hearing Bright's formula, she said, "I'm going to try that." Three months later, she joyfully told me that 12 of the 18 relatives had surrendered their lives to Christ during that short period of time! One couple had even called them long distance to shout, "We're saved! Praise the Lord!"

5. If he isn't antagonistic, share gems you have gotten from your Bible studies with him.
6. Give him intriguing Christian books to read.
7. Go places with him when he asks you, but keep yourself from indulging in sin.
8. Draw the line on anything that would cause you to disobey God.

9. Be loving, beautiful, interesting, and supply his needs eagerly.
10. Don't get so involved in church work that you neglect him or your home.
11. Have a Bible study in your home with a man teacher. A friend of ours who was very anti-God came to Christ that way, after his wife bravely invited the group over.
12. Join with others who have unsaved mates and meet frequently to pray.

15

And Then . . . There Are The Retirement Years

We've had many older couples sparkle up to us announcing that they've been married so many years that there isn't anything that they don't know about each other and nothing new they can learn. We delight with them if theirs has been a happy union, but we don't go along with that adage, "You can't teach an old dog new tricks."

Facing up to the fact that one may NOT have done what he or she should have toward his or her mate all those years is almost too much for the generation that's been there and back again. And yet we find that it's often too true that Dad is no more romantic and attentive now than he was when he was 30 or 40 (usually less so) and Mom has tended to let herself grow "old" when she could have remained young. They have simply adjusted to a less than perfect situation and told themselves it is perfect.

Older couples have asked:

> *You deal with the younger working couples. Will you address the physiological, psychological, sexual and spiritual aspects of the golden years?*

We recognize the fact that there is a difference, but perhaps not as much as you think. If Papa has expected to be waited on all his life, he will expect it even more now. If Momma has spent her life worrying about her children, she'll continue to worry about them now. But at this point they'll both make it more obvious. Uncle Joe will appear to be crankier than when he was younger, Aunt Jane will be more outspoken than ever and offend more people than she used to. That's because they've spent years becoming that way. The true character which has been kept somewhat subdued often shows in the "golden years."

So the same principles that apply for younger couples apply here:

- Take a good look at yourself. Be willing to admit your faults and change them. It's never too late.
- Now that you have extra time, spend a good portion each day in Bible study. We know of several couples who are prayer warriors for others who desperately need their intercession.
- Use your energies to entertain the lonely. Have fun parties.
- Be interested in others of all ages and their activities (not nosy).
- Listen more than you talk.
- Cast any critical attitude you may have right out the window, whether people deserve it or not.
- Husband, be more attentive, romantic and charming to your mate than ever before. Break old, dull habits.
- Wife, be sexy. None of that "too old" nonsense. Keep clean and neat in your person and your home.
- No bellyaching allowed. Sure you've got aches, pains and money troubles. That's your secret. Share it with God.
- Read up on health foods and vitamins and use lots of them.

And remember the old saying: When you laugh the world laughs with you. When you cry, you cry alone.

Our cat is 18 years old. The spit and polish of her younger years has flown the coop and she seems to do nothing these days but eat, sleep, drink and ignore our calls because she's lost her hearing.

Recently, she has been yowling at me everytime I come within sight. From the volume, it's certain she thinks I've lost *my* hearing, too. I check her food, her water, put her in, put her out and still she yowls. Finally, one evening, I let her into our motor home where I was working on this book. She had a wonderful time. She explored every inch and cranny, something I haven't seen her do for a long time. She jumped up and jumped down, sniffed at my typewriter, knocked Chapter Six on the floor and snubbed the dog. I decided she had been BORED.

Don't let boredom happen to YOU. If you have your senses left, don't allow your children to shut you up in a rest home. The ideal is to have a little place of your own, where you can be independent and yet interact with people of all ages. If you are aged, have someone check in on you daily to be sure you haven't fallen or something. If you have to move in with the children, live as separately as possible, do your share of the work as they direct, stay out of their lives and be a joy when you are with them.

P.S. from Margaret: When George's mother passed away, we feared for his stepfather, who had stepped into the position of head of the house when George's Dad died. But Art has been one of those who takes care of himself admirably. He lives alone with his dog and cat, keeps his house, his yard and himself up to snuff. He much prefers it to the idea of coming to live with us. He can do as he pleases, when he pleases. What a life!

16

Perfect Marriage?

Since there are countless UNHAPPY unions, and many people have second and third thoughts about whom they married, it is natural to have them wonder:

Does God consider every marriage as one that is meant to be?

Everyone has as much access to what God considers as we do—in the Holy Bible. We can only be certain of this: God will guide anyone into a relationship that is right if he or she walks very close to Him. We can safely assume that, since we are sin- and self-saturated people, most marriages that do occur weren't "meant" to be by God. If people had allowed Him to run His creation, there would be no divorces, for every match would be perfect. There would be no unhappiness because the world would base its course of action on LOVE, instead of hate and selfishness.

We are happy that such a time is coming, and as the end times draw near, it would be GOOD for you to become knowledgeable regarding prophecy. Check our Bibliography for books which you can read on this subject. You might find that your problems aren't nearly as big as they seem in the light of what is being done eternally.

How long did you work on your marriage to get where you are now?

18 years. Next year, the answer will be 19. Working on personal relationships, going out of your way to be sure love stays warm and vital is an ever-going thing. It's like your relationship with the Lord. When you say "I do" to Christ, you become as strong spiritually as you put time into learning His Word and applying it to your life. You stay as close to Him as the amount of time you spend walking and talking with Him. It's the same with marriage. What went on before you said "I do" as far as love and attention are concerned, should continue to go on after you've left the altar. And in fact, there must be a conscious effort to increase the activity and attitude that went along with your falling in love, if you wish to STAY in love.

Do you feel your marriage is perfect?

Is there anything perfect on the earth? No. Is there *anyone* perfect on the earth? No. Without perfect people, there cannot be a perfect marriage.

But that shouldn't keep anyone from reaching for the stars. AGAPE LOVE hangs there, glistening with sweetness and fatness, just waiting for you to take a big, juicy bite out of it.

AGAPE LOVE is when you give 100% to your mate or others without thought of getting anything in return. Here's a terrific formula to tack up on the wall of your memory and practice daily:

GOD . . . . first
OTHERS . . . . second
ME . . . . last

You'll find that your marriage will soar to eagle heights!

P.S. from both of us: Dear Husband, dear Wife, we know it works, from personal experience and because we have seen it across the land in the lives of the many who have been willing to dive into a new self-less approach to marriage difficulties. You can make it work for you, too.

And the best time to start is now.

BIBLIOGRAPHY

The Authorized King James Version of the Holy Bible, Edited by Rev. C. I. Scofield, D.D. (Old and New Testaments), 1969.

Colson, Charles W., *Born Again*, Chosen Books, Distributed by Fleming H. Revell Company, Old Tappan, New Jersey, 1976.

Davis, Adelle, A.B., M.S., *Let's Eat Right To Keep Fit*, Harcourt, Brace, Jovanovich, Inc., New York, 1970.

Davis, Adelle, A.B., M.S., *Let's Get Well*, Harcourt, Brace & World, Inc., New York, 1965.

Davis, John D., Ph.D., D.D., L.L.D., *The Westminster Dictionary Of The Bible*, The Westminster Press, Philadelphia, 1944.

Dobson, James, Ph.D., *Dare To Discipline*, Tyndale House Publishers, Wheaton, Illinois, 1970.

Eerdmans' Handbook to the Bible, Edited by David Alexander and Pat Alexander, William B. Eerdmans Publishing Company, Grand Rapids, Michigan, 1973.

Hardisty, Margaret E., *Forever My Love*, Harvest House Publishers, Irvine, California, 1975.

Jabay, Earl, *The Kingdom of Self*, Logos International, Plainfield, New Jersey, 1974.

Jones, Charles E., *Life Is Tremendous*, Tyndale House Publishers, Wheaton, Illinois, 1968.

La Haye, Tim, *How To Be Happy Though Married*, Tyndale House Publishers, Wheaton, Illinois, 1968.

Lewin, S. A., M.D., and Gilmore, John, Ph.D., *Sex Without Fear*, Medical Research Press, New York, 1972.

Lindsey, Hal, *The Late Great Planet Earth*, Zondervan Publishing House, Grand Rapids, Michigan, 1970.

Lindsey, Hal, *There's A New World Coming*, Vision House Publishers, Santa Ana, California, 1973.

Miles, Herbert J., Ph.D., *Sexual Happiness In Marriage*, Zondervan Publishing House, Grand Rapids, Michigan, 1968.

Miles, Herbert J., Ph.D., *Sexual Understanding Before Marriage*, Zondervan Publishing House, Grand Rapids, Michigan, 1971.

Morgan, Marabel, *Total Joy*, Fleming H. Revell Company, Old Tappan, New Jersey, 1976.

Narramore, Clyde M., *How To Succeed In Family Living*, Regal Books, Division of G/L Publications, Glendale, California, 1968.

New American Standard Bible, A. J. Holman Company, division of J. B. Lippincott Company, Philadelphia and New York.

The New Testament in Modern English, J. B. Phillips, The MacMillan Company, 1969.

Streshinsky, Shirley, *How Divorce Really Affects Children*, The Redbook Publishing Company, New York, September, 1976.

Strauss, Richard L., *Marriage Is For Love*, Tyndale House Publishers, Wheaton, Illinois, 1973.

Wright, H. Norman, *Communication, Key To Your Marriage*, Regal Books Division, G/L Publications, 1974.

Ziglar, Zig, *There's Room At the Top*, Recorded by Magnemedia, Inc., Irvine, California.

SCRIPTURE REFERENCES